# COACHING FOR

*Why it works and*

# COACHING FOR HEALTH

*Why it works and how to do it*

**Jenny Rogers**
**Arti Maini**

Mc Graw Hill Education  Open University Press

Open University Press
McGraw-Hill Education
McGraw-Hill House
Shoppenhangers Road
Maidenhead
Berkshire
England
SL6 2QL

email: enquiries@openup.co.uk
world wide web: www.openup.co.uk

and Two Penn Plaza, New York, NY 10121-2289, USA

First published 2016

A catalogue record of this book is available from the British Library

ISBN-13: 978-0-33-526230-4
ISBN-10: 0-33-526230-9
eISBN: 978-0-33-526231-1

Library of Congress Cataloging-in-Publication Data
CIP data applied for

Typeset by Aptara, Inc.

# PRAISE FOR THIS BOOK

*"Too often the NHS tells patients how they can improve their health but it falls upon deaf ears. Too often, clinicians advise patients but they don't have the means to effect change. "Coaching for Health" offers a new paradigm. Enabling clinicians and patients to cross that barrier between good intentions and effective action. The authors of this book know their stuff, have walked the talk and this needs to be read by any serious clinician or patient, who wants to make a difference"*
Dr Michael Dixon OBE, GP, former chair of NHS Alliance and
Visiting Professor University College London, UK

*"Most health professionals will be familiar with the idea of coaching as something they or their colleagues might seek, in order to explore their work options or increase their sense of empowerment. In 'Coaching for Health', Jenny Rogers and Arti Maini examine how the coaching model can become something far more than this – an overarching framework for encounters with patients, helping them to share their concerns freely and find ways of resolving them. In a clear and convincing manner, the authors offer a range of practical methods for turning health care consultations into a genuinely patient-led form of dialogue."*
John Launer, Associate Dean for Faculty Development,
Health Education England

*"This is the definitive book on Coaching for Health; I have found it beautifully written. I am so grateful that my vision of changing the mindset from advice-giving to the coaching approach for patient enablement and empowerment has been so skillfully written here by Jenny and Arti, two enormously talented*

people, one a practicing doctor and the other a hugely respected and experienced coach. It uses both theory and practical examples to great effect.

If all medical students were given this to read in their first weeks we could be sure to create a sustainable NHS, with patients more likely to adopt improved healthcare behaviours, be motivated to look after themselves, engage with clinical management plans and to report improved quality of life, even where they have disabling long-term conditions. And clinicians who use coaching with patients will have dramatically reduced stress because the work is so much more satisfying"

*Dr Rebecca Viney, Clinical Advisor Primary Care,*
*Health Education England, UK*

"Jenny Rogers and Arti Maini have put their heads together and come up with a gem of a book. Jenny needs no introduction - her *Coaching Skills: a handbook* is the foundation of any decent coaching library. Arti is a practising GP in London as well as a well-respected coach. The combination of Jenny's accessible style and wisdom with Arti's extensive experience of adopting a coaching approach with patients has produced a winner. The book is studded with examples that spell out how a coaching conversation might go and how it differs from advice-giving, direction or the hard sell. Quotes from clinicians demonstrate how liberating and transformational coaching for health can be for clinicians as well as for patients."

*Lis Paice OBE FRCP, author of New Coach: Reflections from a*
*Learning Journey, UK*

"Supporting self-care effectively is vital to the long term future of health services. This will require a new type of conversation between professionals and patients for which Jenny Rogers and Arti Maini make a convincing case for health coaching. Two particular strengths are the use of narratives and stories - real-life scripts brought to life with colourful examples of coaching in action - and the Q & A in final chapter which answers many of the questions that reader might have about health coaching as an approach. Drawing from range of fields from neuroscience to linguistics, the authors speak to the reader in a positive, *practical and encouraging tone who will undoubtedly feel more 'fired up' to give the coaching approach a go in their next clinic or surgery."*

*Professor Tim Swanwick, Postgraduate Dean, Health Education England, UK*

*The authors bring together in a clear and accessible style the evidence from both the literature and the lived experience of doctors and patients the benefits to be gained from coaching for health. This book is for both the pragmatic and the reflective practitioner – it has an abundance of practical tools, tips, and excellent references, but also thought-provoking ideas and liberating concepts. I highly recommend it for all health care professionals at all stages of their careers as coaching skills can always be honed and refined. In fact, I believe it should be a set book for the undergraduate and postgraduate curricula of all healthcare professionals.*

*Dr Paquita de Zulueta, Honorary Senior Clinical Lecturer, Department of Public Health and Primary Care Imperial College London, UK*

*"Rogers and Maini have skilfully crafted a book which is both easy to read and informative. There is currently unprecedented demand on healthcare systems. The coaching for health approach adds a powerful weapon to the clinician's armamentarium in how to get patients to help themselves in the battle with long term illness. Many compelling examples are given to enhance understanding. This is an excellent book which should be on every clinician's reference list. I am a convert and will definitely push the coaching for health agenda going forward."*

*Dr Caroline Allum, Medical Director Hertfordshire Community Trust, UK*

*"Arti and Jenny raise important questions on how clinicians use coaching skills to create an informed discourse to support patients. By using the principle that 'the purpose of information is a two way process and the meaning of communication is the response we get' they have teased out examples of how 'the gift of the question and a humble inquiry' is able to create a different paradigm.*

*The applications of these principles are applicable in any discipline within healthcare and interestingly the 10-minute consultation does not need to be a limiting factor.*

*This book provides tools with relevant references and would be important reflective reading to any clinician seeking to expand his or her repertoire in the 'art of the consultation.'"*
  *Dr Mohini Parmar, GP and Chair Ealing Clinical Commissioning Group, UK*

*"Those of us who work in clinical practice with all its pressures can struggle to work out how to change the way we act and interact with patients to ensure that the person experiences the best possible quality of life. This book uses practical examples to help in this process. I hope that you find it as useful as I have."*
  *Linda Nazarko, OBE FRCN, Consultant Nurse, UK*

*"All health settings whether a hospital or a GP surgery are places of human distress. Mental Health settings maybe even more so. The coaching approach powerfully creates a space where the options for management and the choices available can be explored in a mutually respectful discussion between clinician and patient, supporting the patient to own their own recovery.*
  *Dr Alex Horne, Consultant Child and Adolescent Psychiatrist, UK*

*"Many health practitioners already use some elements of coaching without realizing it, and this accessible little title will help them further their know-how. Others may be less familiar with the skills, and they can learn all about it here, including the rationale for coaching.*

*The authors explain the application of coaching to different settings, including mental health and the elderly.*

*This realistic guide is for all clinicians, not just for doctors, and I'd recommend it to medical students too. I think it's a game-changer for the consultation, and for the clinician."*
  *Dr Carol Cooper, GP, author, and honorary tutor Imperial College School of Medicine, UK*

*"Primary and community care practitioners, including GPs, will find this book helpful because it shows how to help people to help themselves. By encouraging patients to set their own goals and explore their understanding of the things that are concerning them, coaching helps people to feel more in control of their own destiny. The book contains many useful tips on using language in empowering and healing ways that help patients to manage their anxieties and you to manage yours. Definitely worth having on your shelf."*

Dr Paul Thomas, GP, West London, UK

*"As a clinician and coach I see this beautifully written book as being important for defining and introducing the power of coaching into the clinical consultation and also as the most effective, efficient and engaging conversations we can have with patients. This is something every clinician can learn, reducing stress and increasing satisfaction and enjoyment by enabling and empowering patients in a more meaningful way. The case studies and very natural coaching conversations together bring alive in a most refreshing, realistic and simple way the essence and the effectiveness of coaching style questions in a health care context."*

Dr Elisabeth Hopman, GP, Medical Appraiser and Coach/Mentor, UK

*"An excellent read. I finally know why I have found it difficult to understand some of my most challenging consultations which have left me frustrated. This book is a breakthrough in the art of consulting and provides the necessary tools to make a life-changing difference to the lives of patients. The authors make a persuasive argument in the power of coaching patients which will no doubt lead to long-lasting and sustainable behavioural change. A must read for all doctors."*

Dr Hemal Desai, GP, Medical Leader & Entrepreneur, UK

*"A well-researched and referenced book which shows the reader how to use this powerful technique to more effectively help our patients, and ourselves!*

*Rogers and Maini draw on many theories and distil these into an easy to understand and intuitive model of interaction, ultimately leading to more effective communication which results in safer and better patient care, while at the same time reducing the clinician's levels of stress.*

*Mr Raj Das-Bhaumik, Consultant Ophthalmic, Plastic and Reconstructive Surgeon, Training Director of the Emergency Department, Co-chair of the Moorfields Academy, Moorfields Eye Hospital, UK*

*"Patients at the centre' is a mantra for all clinicians. In this book, the authors use their extensive experience in the field, to clearly explain how Coaching for Health can be used to truly work together with patients to produce change. As well as the obvious uses in lifestyle choices and multimorbidity, complex situations such as disempowered patients and people with long term mental health problems are explored. Filled with clinical vignettes, this is a book for anyone who works with patients, in and out of hospital. Read and be inspired to try out the techniques."*

*Dr Clare Etherington, GP and educator, UK*

*"'Coaching for health' is a practical and well written book with most relevant text illuminating the core of clinical practice – COMMUNICATION.*

*Junior doctors/ nurses and Allied health professionals need this practical knowledge and skill set at their infancy in order to enhance their future careers. It is an essential 'must read' and ought to be incorporated into medical undergraduate/ postgraduate and allied health courses/ curricula.*

*This is an absolutely brilliant piece of work. I found myself able to relate to each theme, clearly and provocatively.*

*AM & JR are to be commended in creating an invaluable tool which will help empower the equal partnership of health professional and patient."*

*Mr Kwamena Amonoo-Kuofi, ENT Consultant, UK*

*From JR: for Samuel*

*From AM: for my parents, my husband and my daughters
Shanti, Ishani and Anisha*

# CONTENTS

# FOREWORD

If you have meningitis how well you do depends on the medical team, whereas if you have diabetes it depends mainly on you, the patient. These days most of health care is about patients with long term conditions, usually multiple conditions. So the old style of health care when sick patients could be rapidly cured, which many health care professionals found deeply satisfying, has been largely replaced by a more complex kind of health care that depends on forming a strong, supportive relationship with patients. Jenny Rogers and Arti Maini call this coaching, and in this book they spell out in practical detail how to coach effectively. Some professionals might find this kind of health care less satisfying, and more frustrating, than the largely extinct curative form, but the book shows how it can be equally and even more satisfying.

Coaching is more a mindset and collection of values than series of techniques, and some of the values, although simple, may prove challenging. The starting assumption is that every patient, no matter how seemingly helpless, can make rational choices and that patients are the experts on themselves. The implication is that patients may make choices very different from those their clinicians would make. The choices may even seem irrational to the clinicians. Even more challenging to some clinicians is that "in a true coaching exchange, the outcome is unknown." It night be the opposite of what clinicians have aimed for.

One reason that the outcome is uncertain is because coaching is a conversation between equals. Clinicians, bristling with degrees and used to exercising authority, must recognise that they are the equals of patients who may have very little education and find it hard to express themselves. And perhaps most challenging of all is the idea that the clinicians may be affected more than the patients by the interaction.

It's very tempting and at first thought quicker to tell patients what to do. This might have worked better in the age of deference, but it probably didn't work well even then. We've long known that many prescriptions are not even taken to the chemist and that adherence rarely rises above 50%. Rogers and Maini quote Angela Coulter, a long term student of clinician patient interactions, that traditional styles of practice "create dependency, discourage self care, ignore patient preferences, undermine patient confidence, do not lead to healthy behaviours, and ultimately lead to fragmented care." What was poor practice in the age of acute, potentially curable disease is disastrous in the age of long term conditions and multimorbidity.

Rogers and Maini are explicit that you cannot learn coaching from a book alone, and it seems to me an activity that can never be perfected: you will keep learning. But the book is full of practical, actionable information.

One of the core skills of coaching is to create the right first impression. As Daniel Kahneman showed in Thinking, Fast and Slow we are hardwired to make almost immediate judgements on people. Clinicians who arrive late, don't smile, don't introduce themselves, and don't look at the patients have a long way to go to build equal, coaching relationships with patients. They start by going backwards.

I much enjoyed the "Rapport checklist" provided by Rogers and Maini: smile; pay close attention to where you place yourself in the room; avoid writing and not looking at the patient; remember non-verbal cues that you are listening, like nodding; use the power of touch judiciously; pay close attention to unspoken nuances in the conversation; and avoid carping and grumbling. We can all benefit from this list in our everyday lives, but the therapeutic power of rapport ("the doctor as drug") should not be underestimated. It's probably one of the reasons that patients are so attracted to complementary practitioners. As Rogers and Maini write: "It is unusual to be offered 100 per cent attention and care by another human being, and it's enormously validating when we do receive it."

The book explores topics where coaching may be especially valuable or particularly difficult or both. Can coaching help people change their behaviours, something that traditionally clinicians do poorly? How can it be useful with disempowered patients, those whom it might be most tempting to tell but who most need a sense that they can control their lives? What are the special aspects of coaching people with mental health problems?

One part of coaching is to identify barriers that patients might feel and experience, and Rogers and Maini end their book by answering the questions that they know clinicians will ask, possibly as a means to resist change. Lack of time is our favourite universal excuse for not doing something, although really it's just saying that the something is not a priority. Will clinicians, particularly GPs with their 10 minute consultations, have time for coaching?

Rogers and Maini's answers are that using some of the basic techniques of coaching are timesaving – like setting the agenda for the consultation, asking patients what they hope to achieve, and summarising what is happening. But they might have answered that the old styles are failing; telling the patient what to do might get them out of the door quickly but will usually not result in improvement. Worse, they may create dependency and undermine self-sufficiency, meaning that the patients may be back soon and often.

After reading the book I was left knowing that I would buy a copy for my daughter who hopes to train as either a doctor or clinical psychologist. Whatever she becomes this book will be useful to her.

Richard Smith
Former editor, BMJ
Chair, Patients Know Best
November 2015

# ABOUT THE AUTHORS

J enny Rogers is internationally known as a teacher, writer, supervisor and speaker on coaching as well as an executive coach with 25 years of experience, and is a full member of the Association for Professional Executive Coaches and Supervisors (APECS). She was a founder-member of the pioneering faculty that developed the London Deanery postgraduate courses on coaching for doctors and has trained many hundreds of clinicians in coaching skills. Her book *Coaching Skills: A Handbook* has become the standard reference text on coaching in the UK and the US. The 5th edition of her classic *Adults Learning*, published in 2008, reflects her long-standing interest in learning and development. She has written best-selling books on the MBTI and FIRO-B psychometric instruments, and is Series Editor of the Coaching in Practice series from the Open University Press. She has also published several books on career themes, is a regular columnist for several magazines and has been a frequent contributor to BBC Radio 4 and the BBC World Service.

Jenny's enthusiasm as a teacher of coaching skills is constantly refreshed and challenged by her own coaching practice where her clients include senior clinicians, chief executives and directors from some of the UK's best known organizations, including many in healthcare.

Arti Maini is a primary care physician and coach. She gained degrees in medicine and in clinical neuroscience from St George's Hospital Medical School in London. She went on to train in general medicine, psychiatry and primary care. She has worked clinically within over a hundred healthcare settings across primary and secondary care since 1999, and has undertaken clinical leadership roles and consultancy work for a range of healthcare organizations. Her passionate interest in learning, development and communication led her to complete an MSc in Medical Education as well as diplomas in Coaching Supervision and in Executive Coaching and Leadership Mentoring. She holds membership of the Royal College of General Practitioners, the International Coach Federation, the Association for Coaching and the Coaching Supervision Academy. She is a Master Practitioner in Neuro-Linguistic Programming, specializing in health and children. She has also trained in health coaching, cognitive behaviour therapy and motivational interviewing, and has developed and taught on communication skills courses at undergraduate and postgraduate levels.

Arti works actively with the NHS London Leadership Academy and with Health Education England as a coach for clinicians. She also works as a coach supervisor and is on the faculty of the Coaching Supervision Academy. She is involved with coaching research and with training clinicians in coaching skills. She first trained in coaching skills in 2001 and since then has regularly incorporated coaching approaches into her own clinical practice with a highly diverse range of patients.

# ACKNOWLEDGMENTS

We thank the many friends, colleagues, patients, clients and clinicians who generously offered us their experiences as case studies in this book. Thanks are also due to the many doctors and other healthcare professionals who have participated in our training courses and given us candid insights into the way it was working out in practice to incorporate a coaching approach into their daily lives.

Two extraordinary women from what was then the London Deanery (now part of Health Education England) dedicated time and energy to establishing and embedding coaching within healthcare settings: Dr Rebecca Viney and Professor Lis Paice had the vision to see how transformative coaching could be, and, with the backing of Dr Tim Swanwick, made sure that an ambitious and innovative programme of training could actually happen. Hundreds of doctors and other healthcare professionals have every reason to be grateful to them, as are we. We also thank Matt Driver and Dr Sue Morrison who worked with us to develop and deliver our training courses for clinicians, and our clinical colleagues from the HENWL Coaching and Mentoring Service who gave skilled and enthusiastic input through facilitating on the courses.

Special thanks are due to Dr Amy Iversen for her invaluable insights and support during the early stages of developing this book. Many others offered us feedback, encouragement and ideas at vital stages, especially Clive Avril, Dr Alex Horne, Jackee Holder, Dr Rosalind Ramsay, Luke Rogers, Jenny Stevens and Dr Thelma Thomas.

Our commissioning editor, Monika Lee of McGraw-Hill Education, has been a steady presence throughout the process of developing and writing this book.

We thank our families, as ever, for their love and belief in us while writing this book:

(AM) My thanks to my parents Kamlesh and Yash Paul Maini, my husband Shanker Vijayadeva, my mother-in-law Geetha Vijayadeva and my daughters Shanti, Ishani and Anisha. They have all in their special and unique ways provided support, encouragement and inspiration.

(JR) My thanks to my sons, their partners and my lovely grandchildren for knowing when to ask exactly the right questions and when to provide delightful distraction.

# INTRODUCTION

Being a clinician is rewarding. You may deservedly earn the heartfelt gratitude of your patients, and you know that what you are doing matters. The work is intellectually and emotionally satisfying. You have opportunities to learn and grow throughout your career.

But being a clinician is also tough. Patients need you, yet they are not always clear about what they need you for. You may do work that makes a difference and even saves lives, but it may be work that leaves you depleted, physically and mentally. You know that many patients need advice on improving their lifestyles or help on deciding between treatment options, or information on medication, yet so many seem to resist your well-meant efforts. You went into your profession for reasons which most probably included a sincere wish to serve others, yet you may feel that you are spending far too much of your time filling in forms and ticking boxes in order to satisfy corporate or government agendas. Of course you know about 'patient-centred practice', but how can this be implemented in an all-too-short consultation with a patient who seems to need a social worker rather than a clinician? How is it possible to stay calm, warm and focused when demand for clinical services is rising at a rate where resources have difficulty keeping up?

We have written this book because of our strong belief that adopting a coaching approach to patient care is one of the most powerful solutions to all of these problems. Our target reader is anyone in a clinical role, whether you are a doctor in an inner-city primary care practice, an orthopaedic surgeon in a busy hospital, a physiotherapist working in sport, a nurse on an oncology ward, a palliative care therapist, pain specialist, dental surgeon, radiographer, podiatrist, occupational therapist, clinical psychologist – the list is virtually limitless. If you work directly with patients then you can use coaching in your clinical practice.

Much of what we describe will be familiar; for instance, all clinicians get at least some training in communication skills. We see coaching as adding to rather than displacing the skills you already have. It is not a panacea because there will be many occasions when a different kind of intervention is needed. We also emphasize throughout the book that coaching is not just a technique that can be switched on and off for the benefit of a few carefully selected patients. It is a wholly different mindset. Yes, there are specific techniques that need to be learnt and practised, but it is when you put them all together that you see how different coaching is.

It starts with the assumption that at some level, regardless of how helpless and dependent they may appear, almost every patient can make rational choices and that it is the patient who is the expert on themselves, not the clinician. The patient's life is lived outside the clinical arena and it is family and friends who will have most potential for support, not the clinician.

Once clinicians begin to realize the power of coaching, they often ask – and they are only half-joking – whether this is just a new and better way of manipulating patients. The question misunderstands what happens to control in a true coaching exchange. Coaching is not a way of secretly holding on to the power while the patient docilely agrees with the outcome you have cunningly planned all along. In a true coaching exchange, the outcome is unknown because it is two people engaged in a different kind of conversation, one that happens between equals, however unequal the relationship may appear on the surface. Coaching assumes that the patient can potentially affect the clinician as much as the clinician affects the patient.

Coaching also accepts that the human approach to change is ambivalent: the bigger the change, the more reluctant we human beings are to make it. This is the opposite of the implicit assumption in so much clinical training, which is that all you have to do is to inform people about what is good for them and they will obediently do it. All clinicians find out early in their careers that this is not what happens and that patients have infinite ways of resisting. Yet the clinician's favourite mode of influencing can still be to tell and advise. This is despite the overwhelming evidence that this strategy is doomed to fail most of the time because it runs counter to one of the main principles of human psychology: when others insist, we resist. Coaching offers a way of recognizing this and of using the alternatives that work, including with those alleged 'heartsink' patients who seem so hard to help.

Coaching will succeed even with patient populations where you might assume that it cannot – for instance, with people who have been diagnosed with severe mental illness, with children, with 'disempowered' patients who have multiple social and medical problems and with people who are reaching the ends of their lives. We give examples of effective practice with all these groups in the chapters that follow.

We are heartened by evidence that we are connecting with so much that is already happening to make coaching an irresistible proposition. It all points in the same direction: the 'patient-centred experience' and 'patient choice' of political discourse; the astounding success of Dr Kate Granger's simple #HelloMyNameIs campaign for more personal rapport with patients; the knowledge that 70 per cent of the healthcare budget is taken up with long-term conditions where the patient's own behaviour is what makes the most difference to the outcomes.

We base what we write in this book on our own lengthy experience, one of us as a doctor and one of us as an executive coach. We also base it on experience of having trained many hundreds of clinicians in coaching, seeing at first hand what they struggle with and then hearing at follow-up days about how transforming it has been to try it out in practice:

> I never understood before about how exploring and agreeing a goal for the consultation radically affects what happens and for the better – it's transformational, no other word for it.

> Self-awareness: never saw that just asking a different type of question will produce totally different results or that trying to stay emotionally cool was counter-productive for me and for the patient.

> Success! Three hardened 'deniers' signed up for the smoking-cessation group! That's in just two weeks.

> I no longer have patients who make me feel helpless, angry and frustrated; I'm learning to face my fears and to trust my patients' resourcefulness .

> 'The System' still feels like a barrier but I've found ways now of incorporating all that tick box stuff into a coaching approach for patients with diabetes and hypertension.

The evidence on coaching for health is still emerging, but increasingly it suggests that it can reach the parts of the human psyche that other approaches cannot. It suggests, for instance, that patients who get coaching are more likely to adopt improved healthcare behaviours, be motivated to look after themselves, engage with clinical management plans and to report improved quality of life, even where they have disabling long-term conditions. Clinicians who use coaching with patients report dramatically reduced stress because the work is so much more satisfying: it enables you to connect with patients in a more authentic way while retaining every aspect of your duty of care and professionalism. There is more on all of this later in the book.

In writing this book we solicited stories from a wide variety of patients. Some of these stories recount the familiar problems of not being heard, of being misunderstood, ignored or bullied. But there are many more which joyfully describe the positive and uplifting experience of being treated in a new way where patient care became entirely a joint enterprise with the clinician. We have matched these patient accounts with quotes from clinicians who have adopted the coaching ethos and have let it permeate everything they do. All these accounts have had identifying detail stripped out of them to protect confidentiality, but in every other way they represent the raw edge of first-hand experience.

Learning the full art of how to become a clinician-coach needs face-to-face training: a book cannot be effective in the same way, but our hope is that it will inspire you to further enquiry, and most importantly of all, to give it a try with your patients.

Jenny Rogers
Arti Maini
August 2015

# 1 COACHING FOR HEALTH: THE TIME IS NOW

In the first decades of the twenty-first century there have been many ideas which encourage patients to be closely involved in the management of their health. There have been whole areas of discussion, training and writing which talk about *the expert patient, patient choice, patient-centred medicine* and *shared decision-making*. Coaching for health draws on all these ideas, yet it is something distinctly different. In this chapter we describe the changes which have made this a development whose time has come.

Here are two versions of the opening phases of a consultation. Assume that in each case the clinician has given a warm greeting to the patient:

---

**Version 1**

| | |
|---|---|
| *Clinician A* | So what can I do for you today? |
| *Patient* | I've come about my husband. I found a stash of empty vodka bottles behind the bins a few days ago and he's drinking far more than he should be. I've tried telling him he should stop |
| *Clinician A* | How much do you reckon he's drinking? |
| *Patient* | At least eight cans of beer every evening but that's when he's home. Sometimes he's already been to the pub |
| *Clinician A* | You should persuade him to stop! |

| | |
|---|---|
| *Patient* | I've tried that and he doesn't listen to me. I've started counting the empty cans and confronting him about them. I've told him about how many units of alcohol a week is a safe number, but he just ignores me |
| *Clinician A* | But, you know, it all depends on him and how much he sees there's a problem. Could you get him to come and see me? |
| Patient | Oh no, whenever I suggest that he just starts swearing and telling me it's none of my business and boasting about how he can hold his drink and that I should stop nagging |
| *Clinician A* | Yes, well we know that just telling problem drinkers to stop doesn't really work and what does [embarks on a lengthy description of treatment options for addictions.] |

This conversation focuses largely on the person who is not in the room – the patient's husband. As it goes on its well-intentioned way, the clinician will most probably be doing more and more of the talking, taking more and more of the responsibility for the outcome and the patient will be doing less of the talking and most probably listening less. The real problem may or may not emerge later and may be much more time-consuming to resolve in the longer term.

| | |
|---|---|
| **Version 2** | |
| *Clinician B* | So what do you need to get out of this consultation? |
| *Patient* | [hesitantly] It's about my husband... |
| *Clinician B* | Your husband...? |
| *Patient* | Yes, he's drunk every night, [long pause] he's so aggressive with me, tells me I'm nagging him |
| *Clinician B* | Aggressive – that sounds tough, very difficult for you. I'm sorry to hear it. What do you mean by aggressive? |

| Patient | [tremulously] I'm afraid he's going to hit me again – he did last week when he'd already been to the pub on his way home from work then drank about seven cans of beer and got totally paralytically drunk and when I told him he shouldn't be drinking so much and reminded him he'd promised to stop, and that I'd found empty vodka bottles behind the bin... [breaks down] |
|---|---|
| Clinician B | Take your time... |
| Patient | He slapped me really hard and I fell against the wall, then later, well next day actually, he cried and said he was sorry... |
| Clinician B | Very very difficult for you. What do you need from me today? |
| Patient | I need to know what I can do to stop this happening again, and whether there's any way of stopping him carrying on like this – his liver must be half destroyed already because he's been a heavy drinker as long as I've known him |
| Clinician B | So there are two things we need to discuss here: how to stop him from attacking you again – and I need to check in a minute whether this has left you with any injury we need to deal with – and what might persuade him to give up or moderate his drinking. Is that right? |
| Patient | Yes, yes, that's it! |

Version 2 is the coaching approach. The clinician asks the patient what her goal is for the consultation, so the patient is setting the agenda; by asking her to focus on the heart of her concerns she is more likely to be able to state them straight away and the discussion is more likely to meet her needs. The clinician has picked up on the patient's language and takes care to express rapport. The patient will feel heard and so it will be easier for her to say what is really on her mind. The clinician checks back with the patient on whether the agenda is the right one, and there may be a point later in the conversation where she is offered a choice about which of the topics to pursue that day and which might be the focus of a subsequent consultation. The balance of talking and listening is likely to be evenly spread between both parties. This approach is more likely to be successful: it will get to the core of what the patient needs, will use the time more effectively and is more likely to be a positive experience for patient and clinician.

## What do patients actually do with the information and advice that clinicians give them?

Coaching for health is a new way of interacting with patients. You will most likely know of stories like these, all of which suggest that change is needed:

> After Bob died, his sister discovered five bulging bags under his bed. They contained the medication he had been prescribed over the years of his illness. It looked as if he had dutifully collected all his drugs but had taken none, as every package was intact.

> Cynthia has just come home from a visit to the diabetes specialist nurse. When her son asks her how she got on, she shakes her head saying she's not quite sure. Cynthia was told that she is 15 kilos over the ideal weight for her height and age and that she has a body mass index of 35. She was unable to take in any more of the conversation, though she nodded politely at various stages of it, because she doesn't know how kilos compare with stones and pounds, nor what body mass index is.

> Marietta has rheumatoid arthritis and high cholesterol levels. Her doctor has told her it would be advisable to go on statins along with the other drugs she is taking. After experiencing some unpleasant side effects, Marietta gets three different sets of advice from her hospital consultant, family doctor and pharmacist, so she makes a unilateral decision to stop taking the statins.

> Al has already guessed that his cardiac surgeon will recommend a particular operation and comes to his outpatient appointment with a printout of internet comments about one aspect of its safety. The surgeon smiles, waves a hand airily and says, 'Leave me to worry about that'.

> Ted has had two fractures in quick succession, has a copy of his DEXA scan and knows he has osteoporosis. As he waits for the first meeting at the hospital, he is handed a short questionnaire to fill in about his lifestyle. There is a brief exchange of pleasantries as

the doctor welcomes him and glances quickly at the results. Then she launches into a little talk on nutrition, including the importance of limiting alcohol consumption and including enough calcium and oily fish in his diet. Ted half-listens, too annoyed to interrupt and tell her that although officially retired, he is still an internationally recognized expert on nutrition and probably knows more than she does about the nuances of diet in cases of osteoporosis.

These stories illustrate what we already know from research. Half of patients leave visits to primary care not having understood what their doctor or nurse has told them. Although it is well established that shared decision-making improves outcomes, only 9 per cent of patients say they participated in decisions about their health. Average adherence rates for prescribed medications are around 50 per cent: one recent survey estimated that £300 million was wasted in England alone on medication that was collected from the pharmacy but never taken or finished. When clinicians suggest lifestyle changes to reduce the impact of illness, only 10 per cent of patients follow their advice.[1-3]

We need the coaching approach in healthcare because the entire health landscape has changed. The old models of what it means to be a clinician are under pressure in virtually every part of the world. There are innumerable factors shaping these changes, many of them driven by technological and social developments.

## Patients are less patient

Patients are far less likely to be docile than was once the case. Clinicians no longer have exclusive control over medical information. Patients commonly bring along sheaves of papers they have downloaded from the internet; such information may or may not be accurate or helpful, but it changes the dynamic of the conversation. Pharmaceutical companies now advertise prescription drugs direct to patients in many countries, hoping that the patient will put pressure on the doctor to prescribe. These are just some of many ways in which patients are no longer the meek recipients of care that they may once have been. We are better educated, with roughly 40 per cent of all 18-year-olds now enrolling for higher education in most First World countries[4] – and better education brings more confidence and more willingness to challenge. There is less automatic respect for authority; it has to be earned and depends more on moral authority than on hierarchical position.

Social, economic and technological change have all played their part in creating a society where participation and feedback are the norm. We fill in online surveys on everything from whether the telecoms engineer was prompt and polite when restoring our broadband service to what we think of our local medical practice. Going to a theatrical performance may involve live, improvised interaction with the actors in the same way that we might take part in a focus group which mixes clinicians, patients and carers at our local hospital. Services that used to be provided for us we now provide for ourselves, whether it is booking our own holidays online or using mobile technology in a remote rural area to send health data to a doctor many miles away.

## Patients in control

There is now an impressive momentum towards putting patients in control of their own health. In one sense this merely recognizes the reality that as patients we may spend perhaps 9,000 hours of our year managing our health in our own homes, and on average fewer than 5 hours with health professionals. The need for patient involvement has been given many names: *patient activation, patient-centred medicine, the expert patient, patient self-management, self-monitoring* and so on. It may also be what is implied by the phrase *patient choice*, though in practice that seems to mean giving patients a choice of provider rather than putting them in charge of the management of their own health. Summing up many dozens of similar calls for action in medical journals and books, the King's Fund[5] commented in 2014:

> A shift is also needed to involve patients much more closely in decisions about their care. It is time to make shared decision-making between doctors and patients a reality; when patients are fully informed about their options, they often choose different and fewer treatments. The NHS should make better use of data and technology to support patients in managing their own care.

In a conference sponsored by the East of England Deanery, Angela Coulter, Director of Global Initiatives for Informed Medical Decision-Making, Boston, and Senior Research Scientist at the Department of Public Health at the University of Oxford, gave a lecture entitled 'What patients want from talking to their clinicians'. Her conclusions were that traditional practice styles create dependency, discourage self-care, ignore patient preferences, undermine patient confidence, do not lead to healthy behaviours and ultimately lead to fragmented care.[6]

In most Western countries healthcare has been largely based on a now outmoded model, where episodic visits to hospitals form its apex with the spotlight on crisis. The discourse now is about how services can be centred firmly on a community model and where it also seems that the unhappy child of medicine, public health, is due to come into its own with far more emphasis on prevention and education.

## The smartphone revolution

In a sense, much of the discussion about patient involvement already seems quaintly out of date and set to become even more so. Digital technology is rapidly disrupting the traditional clinician–patient relationship because it has the potential to put data and diagnosis in the hands of any patient who wants it. This may be unmediated by a clinician and also allows patients to connect with one another and to research their own conditions. Digital technology gives patients the equivalent of a university research library, a printing press and a community of other patients at the swipe of a finger or the click of a mouse. This is already how it works in many other sectors – for instance, banking, retail, entertainment, stock markets, transport, holidays. At the last count, one in four of the world's population possessed a smartphone and connections to broadband internet are now available in even the most remote parts of the world.[7]

In his book *The Patient Will See You Now: The Future of Medicine is in Your Hands*,[8] Dr Eric Topol, a distinguished cardiologist, describes using his smartphone with sensors to diagnose people who were facing medical emergencies on planes. He comments that any flight attendant with a smartphone plus sensor and app could have done exactly what he did, including making reliable recommendations about whether the plane needed to make an emergency landing or not.

Here are just some of the scenarios that are now possible with smartphone technology, all of which have the potential to put patients in the position where they can manage their own health, often sidestepping the need for some of the traditional clinician skills:

- Using the camera on your phone to take a picture of a skin condition, downloading an app which delivers an accurate diagnosis together with recommendations for treatment, which may or may not involve a visit to a doctor.
- Measuring your own vital signs: blood glucose, blood pressure, heart, lungs, including worrying symptoms which suggest that an emergency admission is essential. With the right sensors and apps, the phone delivers an accurate diagnosis based on a sophisticated algorithm. This potentially bypasses one of the clinician's most treasured skills: the ability to diagnose.
- Conveying lab test results direct to the patient's phone without having to go through the intermediary of a doctor's office. Patients no longer have to beg to see their own data.
- Patients accessing their data directly. If it contains unflattering or inaccurate references to their personality or circumstances, they could edit it.
- Patients connecting with each other, for instance through powerful sites such as PatientsLikeMe.com where they can be certain that there will be no disapproval, can exchange stories for support and can access high-quality research.
- Patients with extremely rare conditions doing the complex and time-consuming research which uncovers the causes of their disease, and then, using social media, publicizing their findings to anyone interested.
- Wearing devices: watches, pedometers, sleep monitors and so on all put the individual in a position of mastery over their own activity. The number of such devices that each of us owns is likely to increase. If they wish, patients can send this data direct to a clinician, so, for instance, a physiotherapist could review a patient's rehab progress in real time.

These developments create new challenges for twenty-first-century healthcare; by welcoming such phenomena and learning how to work with them to add value, clinicians are likely to create more engaged patients.

## The complementary health phenomenon

In the last 30 years there has been an upsurge of interest in complementary and alternative approaches to health. Specialist chains of shops sell vitamin and mineral supplements as well as 'natural' remedies for menopausal symptoms, weight loss, arthritis, loss of libido, depression, anxiety and other conditions. There is reflexology, acupuncture, hypnotherapy, homeopathy, Ayurvedic medicine, Chinese medicine, osteopathy – many available on any high street or in any shopping mall, some regulated and staffed by well-trained practitioners, some not. Public interest and support for these approaches may in part represent a frustration with how patients experience mainstream healthcare. Patients want someone who will listen with warmth, give them time, take them seriously, treat them as equals – all qualities they may feel are lacking when they visit a clinician who is palpably buckling under the pressure of seeing too many patients for too short a time.

## The impact of health 'scandals'

Media exposures of poor practice have played their part in damaging automatic respect for the clinical professions. Over the last decades of the twentieth century and the first two of the twenty-first century, there has been a steady stream of revelations about unethical or poor clinical performance. It is worth noting that many of these scandals have been triggered not by journalists or fellow clinicians, but by members of the public, troubled or outraged by what they have experienced or observed. Shockingly poor standards have been uncovered in large hospitals such as Stafford in England, where between 2005 and 2008 several hundred more patients died than would have been expected at a hospital of its type. A local campaigner whose mother had died at the hospital revealed the appalling extent of abuse and neglect by nursing staff and incompetence from the hospital's management: all of this was widely and indignantly reported where previously it might have been hushed up. The revelation of these shameful failures of care was a transformative moment for the National Health Service in the UK, showing how easily standards can slip. The subsequent Francis Report[9] triggered massive changes in the inspection regime, a new duty of candour, and a number of initiatives to make more information available to the public about how services perform.

## Transparency

All the clinical professions are more transparent than they used to be even ten years ago, and this transparency can diminish the automatic respect that many of them, especially medicine, used to enjoy. Reports of fitness to practise proceedings can be freely read in newspapers or on websites, and the regulators' own performance is also open to public assessment. Patient surveys can reveal areas of chronic dissatisfactions with care. Where hospital staff respond negatively to survey questions about whether they would recommend their own organization to friends and family, the statistics will be copiously reported. The results of inspection visits by regulators are often leaked even before the final report has been written.

Just as we expect to be able to make choices about something trivial such as the best refrigerator or something important such as the best schools for our children, we also expect to be treated as consumers in healthcare. In the twenty-first century there is more willingness to comment in public about personal encounters, whether through a well-considered blog on an individual website or through impulsive posts on Twitter or Facebook. Nor are such comments necessarily made in anger: there is a rise in the numbers of people who will say that they are making their complaints for altruistic reasons so that others do not have to go through similarly unpleasant experiences.

We are more impatient with waiting, a phenomenon that is often reinforced through formally imposed targets, whether it is to get seen within a few hours in accident and emergency departments or within a maximum number of weeks for surgery. We are less tolerant of behaviour in clinicians which could be seen as incompetent, poorly communicated, discourteous or dismissive; we will complain more readily and may not be easily fobbed off. It is also much simpler to complain than it ever has been in the past: where a complaint might have been dismissed for lack of evidence previously, some patients will now make secret recordings to boost their case. All of this helps account for the steep rise in complaints over fitness to practise in every clinical discipline.

## In their own words: clinicians are human

We should not underestimate the impact it can make when clinicians write, tweet or blog about the experience of doing their jobs. The US surgeon and writer Atul Gawande has written compellingly about the need for greater humility and openness to feedback in medical professionals. His article in the *New Yorker*[10] describes how, as a successful surgeon in mid-career, he asked a distinguished former teacher, now retired, to watch him operate and then to give him feedback and coaching on what he had observed:

> That one twenty-minute discussion gave me more to consider and work on than I'd had in the past five years. It had been strange and more than a little awkward having to explain to the surgical team why Osteen was spending the morning with us. 'He's here to coach me,' I'd said. Yet the stranger thing, it occurred to me, was that no senior colleague had come to observe me in the eight years since I'd established my surgical practice. Like most work, medical practice is largely unseen by anyone who might raise one's sights. I'd had no outside ears and eyes.

The well-known neurosurgeon Henry Marsh published his book *Do No Harm*[11] in 2014 to some astonishment from fellow doctors at his candour. The book has been a bestseller. In his introduction he says his motives for writing it were to 'help people understand the difficulties – so often of a human rather than a technical nature – that doctors face'. The book describes the stress of the work, the impossibility of offering a long-term cure to so many patients with brain tumours, the multiple quiet triumphs along with the occasional devastating failures that could put patients into long-term vegetative states. He also describes delivering a lecture in America to fellow surgeons entitled 'All my worst mistakes' which, he dryly comments, 'was met by a stunned silence and no questions were asked. For all I know they may have been stunned not so much by my reckless honesty as by my incompetence.'

## Clinician stress

Social, economic and political changes have created new challenges for clinicians. Clinicians are likely to experience stress when there is a clash between what their environment needs and how they perceive their own personal resources to meet those needs, especially where they believe they have low levels of control over their work.

Another issue relates to the immense sense of responsibility clinicians may often feel for the patient's well-being. If this gets out of control, you can feel that you are never good enough, leading to high levels of stress.

Knowing how easily a disaffected patient can complain adds stress to an already stressful job. Dealing with a complaint is a dismaying and time-consuming experience, distracting attention from the core purpose of the clinical role, let alone the rising cost of indemnity insurance. Fear of complaints can lead clinicians to more 'defensive' practice, such as more unnecessary referrals, more unnecessary antibiotics prescribing, more unnecessary paperwork.

Introducing a survey on the impact on doctors of being the focus of a complaint,[12] the British Medical Association's (BMA) Doctors for Doctors Unit head, Dr Michael Peters said:

> Doctors are often terrified about complaints. If a doctor has a complaint made against them, it goes into their psyche. It is not like being an accountant who slips up; it can mean the destruction of a whole person. That is how the doctor perceives it.

Henry Marsh[11] makes the same point, describing his rapid descent into fear when he receives a letter from a solicitor threatening a lawsuit:

> I am forced to see the great distance beneath the rope on which I am balancing and the ground below. I feel as though I am about to fall into a frightening world where the usual roles are reversed – a world in which I am powerless and at the mercy of patients who are guided by suave, invulnerable lawyers who, to confuse me even further, are dressed in respectable suits just as I am and speak in the same self-confident tones. I feel that I have lost all credibility and authority that I wear like an armour when I do my round on the wards or when I open a patient's head in the operating theatre.

## Demographic change makes the clinician's job more challenging

Demographic change has added to the challenge. Wars, economic pressures and migration have produced highly diverse populations, ethnically and culturally, all over the world – in all the clinical professions and in the population at large. Language barriers may impede good-quality communication, and patients may sometimes struggle to get the access they need to clinical care. Along with rising numbers of prosperous people, in many countries there are worryingly large numbers of people who are marginalized and living in poverty. As a clinician you may feel you have to work harder to help such people and that it takes more self-management to control your own feelings of despair, impatience or shock when you understand what such patients deal with on a daily basis.

The numbers of people with long-term conditions such as diabetes, cardiovascular disease, depression and arthritis are steeply increasing, partly because people are living longer. Along with this lengthening lifespan goes the probability of accompanying complex medical problems, so for instance an 85-year-old patient may have osteoarthritis, Parkinson's disease and hypertension. Something like 70 per cent of the healthcare budget is absorbed by treating long-term conditions. In 2008 there were 1.8 million people in the UK with long-term conditions, but by 2018 it is estimated that this will have increased to 2.9 million.[13]

Poor lifestyle choices mean that there are rising numbers of people with preventable conditions caused, for instance, by obesity, smoking, lack of exercise or alcohol misuse. There is a sensible expectation that clinicians can or should be able to play a part in prevention and control here, but what will help such patients? There is a plethora of research[14] showing the ineffectualness of just giving people booklets, chiding them with lectures or handing out a prescription where the patient's opinions and needs are neither sought nor taken into account.

All of this would be hard enough, but scientific advances have vastly increased the options for the treatment and management of disease, meaning that diagnosing and prescribing are no longer the more straightforward processes that they were even 20 years ago. Deciding what to do is more complicated and the risks are greater. As the distinguished medical academic Professor Sir Cyril Chantler[15] famously said, 'Medicine used to be simple, ineffective and relatively safe. It is now complex, effective and potentially dangerous.' From the clinician's point of view, it is not surprising that many report being under significant stress.

Clinicians will commonly describe their own frustration when it seems that they are unable to fulfil the drive to help people which took them into clinical practice in the first place. Physicians will, for instance, describe patients with multiple social problems and with symptoms that cannot be explained by any current diagnosis, yet who turn up frequently wanting and needing help.

In the past, much care was in reality only available from Monday to Friday, with sketchy services available at weekends, whether in primary or secondary care. Yet demand for healthcare is rising steadily, at a time when budgets are being capped or cut. Now the mantra of '24/7' access to healthcare is likely to increase the sense of strain. Clinicians are under pressure to deliver more with less. Any such clinician will need to know how to work with patients on treatment options or on how to explain complex procedures in ways that go beyond the platitudes of 'patient choice'.

## What keeps the system stuck?

When it seems so obvious that it is perfectly possible to offer discerning, compassionate care based on empathy and on the recognition that the patient is an equal, how is it that so much of the old behaviour persists? *All too easily* seems to be the answer.

First, there is the challenge of doing work that has been well described as *emotional labour*: it can only be done effectively by engaging heart as well as mind, and when you are working with sick, frightened people, dealing every day with the unpleasantness of disease – the look, the smell, the sound – it takes enormous self-possession and moral courage to respond with empathy and not disgust or fear at the daily reminder of your own mortality. A classic study of student nurses carried out more than 45 years ago by Isabel Menzies Lyth[16] is still relevant today. Nurses operated in a punitive climate, learned to repress emotion, were encouraged to carry out rote tasks unthinkingly, were reluctant to make decisions and learned to think of the patient as a case: a diseased organ rather than as an individual. These were all defences against the personal cost of becoming 'involved'. Now, as then, we see that these defences are bought at a high price: burnout, disengagement, mental illness, high levels of sickness absence and often ultimately the abandonment of a clinical career.

Just as important is the feeling, reported by so many clinicians, of working in a system which begins to seem like a factory where there are too few workers and where efficiency is the only thing that appears to matter. When this happens you carry out rote tasks robotically, depersonalizing patients, for instance referring to patients as 'Bed 8', or repressing emotion when you witness a patient dying. The comments of these clinicians are all too typical of what can happen to compassion in such situations:

It almost becomes a game to get the patients sorted as quickly as possible and get them out of hospital, trying and inevitably failing to get through countless tasks on the job list – because the list is never-ending when new patients are being admitted and there are not enough staff to deal with them.

Really, the way to survive seemed to be to depersonalize the patients and myself – this would get the job done quickest – though being a robot was literally soul destroying.

I couldn't allow myself what seemed like the luxury of empathizing – I had to get through my shift, enter my notes, get on to the next task.

The Royal College of Nursing response[17] to the Francis Report sums it up: 'Through constant change, chronic understaffing and unrelenting pressure, staff have had kindness and compassion eroded from them.'

An article in the UK's *Nursing Times* referred to a study suggesting that nurses have higher levels of stress than troops in combat zones.[18] The article drew many online comments, including this one from an anonymous nurse:

Recently I came home from a 12 hour shift, exhausted, and cried for half hour in front of my husband, who could not console me ... Why ... Because it was another shift on a busy, female surgical ward and even though I had given 110% of my time, energy, I still felt guilty when a relative was upset because her relative looked *uncared for*, even though we were looking after and caring for this patient [who had dementia], who needed all care on a ward with surgical patients coming back from theatre needing post op care. I've lost count the amount of times I've left the ward an hour after the shift finished! I live 23 miles' drive from the hospital and got home about 9:20pm after working from 7am, and what are we told by the managers, you must finish 7:30pm because you will not get time back!! Unfortunately we as nurses care ... And always will about our patients.

Politicians know that healthcare is a vital preoccupation for most of us, so they fear the wrath of the electorate and institute targets, controls, systems, looking for measurable outcomes – even though so many of the things that matter most in healthcare are intangible and can never be measured. It is difficult for politicians and senior managers in health-care to accept that control is a delusion, along with predictability. A system that deliberately encourages competition instead of collaboration and where healthcare is assumed to be a commodity that can be traded, with 'efficiency' as the treasured feature, will put compassion last and the appearance of competence first.

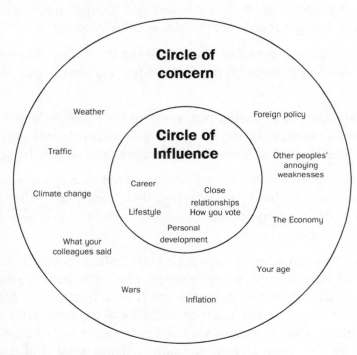

**Figure 1.1** The circle of concern and the circle of influence
Source: Adapted from Covey, *The 7 Habits of Highly Effective People.*[19]

Thus many of the clinicians we know will describe working to a daily ritual of tasks assigned by others, of sitting at a computer endlessly recording processes in time that could be better spent with patients. Fear is pervasive: fear of blame, fear of risk, fear of taking responsibility, becoming skilled at delegating everything upwards. In these taxing circumstances it can be hard to see that even in the most stringently demanding circumstances, there is virtually always something that it is within individual clinician's control. The art is in being able to define what is and is not within your influence. When clinicians burn out or rust out it is often because they expend inordinate amounts of energy on areas where they can have no influence and underestimate the size of the area where they can have influence. One way of looking at this is to consider a comparison between your circle of concern and your circle of influence (Figure 1.1).[19] The circle of concern represents issues over which we can have no control: wars, crime levels, foreign policy, economic trends. The circle of influence is all those issues which we can affect: our own behaviour, our immediate environment, the daily choices we make.

If your mental circle of concern is large but your circle of influence is small (Figure 1.2), this is a recipe for stress. It is far less stressful when the proportion of the two circles is the other way round, that is, when the circle of concern is small and the circle of influence is large (Figure 1.3), because it is much better to expend energy on the areas where individual control is possible. It is true that the systemic issues are very real and need addressing, but also that on an individual level we need to explore what part we have some control and responsibility over, and work with that. When this happens it will result in a more resilient workforce, not slaves to the system or to burnout, and to more meaningful and rewarding work with patients. We know this is the case through our work in coaching doctors and other healthcare professionals where, even in the most dire of situations, they have been able to

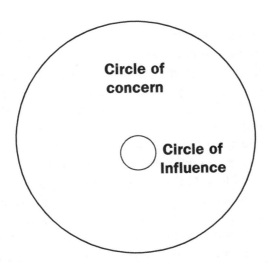

**Figure 1.2** Small circle of influence, large circle of concern: recipe for stress.
Source: Adapted from Covey, *The 7 Habits of Highly Effective People.*[19]

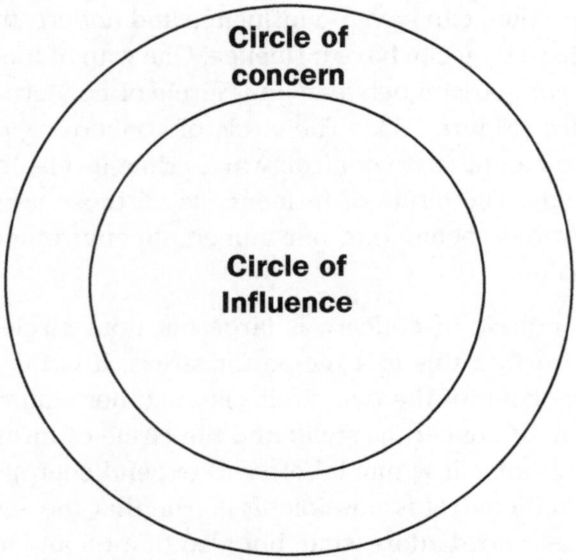

**Figure 1.3** Large circle of influence, small circle of concern: recipe for resilience
Source: Adapted from Covey, *The 7 Habits of Highly Effective People.*[19]

identify something that is within their control and that would make a difference.

## Summary

There is formidable momentum towards a different kind of interaction between patient and clinician. Patients are more confident, better educated, expect participation in decisions about their health and have easy access to information previously confined to clinical professionals. Well publicized failures in regulation have lessened the automatic respect that many clinical professionals enjoyed in the past. Demographic changes have increased the numbers of people with long-term conditions where improved lifestyle management could have a positive impact on quality of life. At the same time many of these patients may have complex conditions, making prescribing and treatment options more complex. Much of this has contributed to reportedly high levels of clinician stress. A large amount of research has shown that traditional tell-and-prescribe models have limited effectiveness. In the next chapter we set out our own definition of what coaching for health is and why it may be at least part of the solution to some of these problems.

# References

1. Health Education East of England. *Health Coaching Interim Progress Report.* https://eoeleadership.hee.nhs.uk/sites/default/files/1404813191_LmkH_health_coaching_interim_progress_report.pdf (accessed 7 June 2015).
2. World Health Organization. Adherence to Long Term Therapies: Evidence for Action. http://www.who.int/chp/knowledge/publications/adherence_report/en/ (accessed 13 August 2015).
3. Trueman, P., Taylor, D.G., Lowson, K., Bligh, A., Meszaros, A., Wright, D. and Glanville, J. *Evaluation of the Scale, Causes and Costs of Waste Medicines: Final Report.* York: York Health Economics Consortium and London: The School of Pharmacy, University of London; 2010. http://discovery.ucl.ac.uk/1350234/ (accessed 13 August 2015).
4. Moynagh, M. and Worsley, R. *Changing Lives, Changing Business: Seven Life Stages in the 21st Century.* London: A&C Black; 2009.
5. The Kings Fund. *Improving Quality of Care.* http://www.kingsfund.org.uk/topics/general-election-2015/priorities-next-government/improving-quality-care. (accessed 3 May 2015).
6. Coulter, A. What patients want from talking to their clinicians. Presented at Talking Differently: Health Coaching for Person-Centred Care and Behaviour Change Conference, Thetford; 2014. https://eoeleadership.hee.nhs.uk/healthcoaching_conference
7. eMarketer. *Worldwide Smartphone Usage to Grow 25% in 2014.* http://www.emarketer.com/Article/Worldwide-Smartphone-Usage-Grow-25-2014/1010920. (accessed 7 May 2015).
8. Topol, E. *The Patient Will See You Now: The Future of Medicine is in Your Hands.* New York: Basic Books; 2015.
9. Francis, R. *Report of the Mid Staffordshire NHS Foundation Trust Public Inquiry.* London: The Stationery Office; 2013.
10. Gawande, A. Personal best. The *New Yorker*, 3 October 2011. http://www.newyorker.com/magazine/2011/10/03/personal-best (accessed 9 May 2015).
11. Marsh, H. *Do No Harm.* London: Orion; 2014.
12. BMA. *BMA Launches Complaints Survey.* http://bma.org.uk/news-views-analysis/news/2012/november/bma-launches-complaints-survey (accessed 3 June 2015).
13. Department of Health. *Long Term Conditions Compendium of Information* (3rd edition); 2012. https://www.gov.uk/government/publications/long-term-conditions-compendium-of-information-third-edition (accessed 11 May 2015).
14. The Health Foundation. *Helping People Help Themselves*; 2011. http://www.health.org.uk/sites/default/files/HelpingPeopleHelpThemselves.pdf (accessed 13 August 2015).
15. Chantler, S.C. Soundbites. *British Medical Journal* 1998; 317(7173): 1666.
16. Menzies Lyth, I. The functions of social systems as a defence against anxiety: A report on a study of the nursing service of a general hospital. *Human Relations* 1959; 13: 95–121. Reprinted in *Containing Anxiety in Institutions: Selected Essays, vol. 1.* London: Free Association Books; 1988, pp. 43–88.

17. Royal College of Nursing. *Mid Staffordshire NHS Foundation Trust Public Inquiry Report; Response of the Royal College of Nursing.* https://www.rcn.org.uk/__data/assets/pdf_file/0004/530824/francis_response_full_FINAL.pdf. (accessed 11 June 2015).
18. Calkin, S. Nurses more stressed than combat troops. *Nursing Times,* 15 January 2013. http://www.nursingtimes.net/nursing-practice/specialisms/management/nurses-more-stressed-than-combat-troops/5053522.article (accessed 11 June 2015).
19. Covey, S.R. *The 7 Habits of Highly Effective People, Powerful Lessons in Personal Change.* New York: Simon & Schuster; 1990.

# 2 THE COACHING MINDSET

I n the last few years the whole idea of *coaching for health* has taken off as a cheap, sustainable and simple solution for some of the issues we described in the previous chapter. In this chapter we define what coaching for health is, what its core principles are and how it differs from some of the other approaches to which it is closely related. We have called this the 'coaching mindset' as a way of emphasizing that coaching for health is about a whole set of values rather than just a toolkit of techniques.

The word *coaching* can be misleading or baffling because it is used in so many different ways. To take one example, it is used in sport to describe a number of processes which in practice can have significantly different shades of meaning. So, for instance, a football coach is often a commanding figure who acts as team manager with the power to choose the team, decide on the training regime and hire other coaches in support roles. The word *coaching* is used by the tutor you might hire to teach your child as preparation for public examinations; and it is also used as a synonym for *mentoring*, implying receiving benign advice and possibly patronage from someone more senior in the same organization. The word has been adopted by a number of other professionals, so you might encounter a debt coach (formerly a debt adviser), a relationship coach (a new term for a marital counsellor), a parenting coach or even, as seen at an exhibition once, a flirting coach.

## The origins of health coaching

Coaching for health has emerged from multiple sources. One of the most influential strands in its development has been psychological therapy in all its many forms, from psychoanalysis to cognitive behavioural therapy (CBT). Starting in the late nineteenth century with radical thinkers such as Sigmund Freud, and now with several hundred rival theories and new ones sprouting all the time, therapy has helped us understand that psychological misery can create mental illness as severely handicapping as physical disease and that body and mind are linked. It has demonstrated the curative power of talking to a trained listener.

In the 1970s and 1980s, some of these influences came together in the *Human Potential Movement* based at the Esalen Institute in California. This movement itself grew out of the *counterculture* thinking of the 1960s. The essential ideas were that human beings have the potential to grow and develop, that we are all intrinsically resourceful and know the answers to our own problems.

The Human Potential Movement paralleled and influenced the development of new approaches to therapy, such as *person-centred therapy* and *transactional analysis.* If you want to do good in the world but believe that people are flawed, broken and helpless, then you will be driven by a need to rescue and reform – and deeply puzzled by why the recipients of your efforts are not more appreciative or compliant. If, on the other hand, you believe that people are resourceful and can make soundly based decisions for themselves, then you will see your professional role as one that involves facilitating other people's thinking rather than imposing your own.

This philosophy was given additional momentum by the emergence of *positive psychology* in the 1990s, an approach which is about working from strengths where the focus is on happiness and well-being, rather than dysfunction where the emphasis is on weakness. The ideas of positive psychology were given a boost through the work of the influential American psychologist, educator and writer, Martin Seligman. He developed the concept of *learned helplessness*, something he said he often saw in people with depression, whose experiences appeared to have taught them that there was nothing they could do to control or improve their lives, even when there were actually opportunities to do so. He offered the notion of *learned optimism* as an alternative. Positive psychology represented a step change. Previously, there was a tendency to assume that contentment meant the absence of misery. Now we can see that psychological well-being is associated with a sense of personal mastery, of accepting yourself, having rewarding relationships and feeling that you have a purpose in life. You can visit Martin Seligman's website[1] for an overview of his ideas, books and other resources, including free questionnaires.

## The influence of executive coaching

Many of the people who met and studied at Esalen went on to become the first executive coaches, including Sir John Whitmore ,whose book *Coaching for Performance*,[2] originally published in 1992, was an early example of how coaching could be a formidable development tool for leaders.

Executive coaching recognizes that leadership roles are stressful, demanding and can be lonely. When you get promotion into the most senior levels of an organization it can be a shock to discover that the job needs a new set of skills, not just the old skills used on a slightly bigger scale in the new environment. People in such jobs mostly do not need to go on training courses, but they often do need and appreciate high-level, one-to-one challenge and support. Most FTSE 500 companies in the UK or Fortune 500 companies in the USA as well as most large public sector organizations now offer executive coaching to their most senior employees. The coach is usually external to the organization and brings psychological know-how, coaching skills and business nous to the relationship. It is confidential, frank, intense, challenging and closely tailored to what the client and the organization need. Aims will usually include raising self-awareness, developing skills and increasing the person's capacity to reach their potential.

Most executive coaches will take a whole-person approach – that is, they will explore personal as well as professional relationships. Like every other kind of coaching, its roots are complex: religion, philosophy, medicine, neuroscience, management and leadership development, sport, psychometrics, organization behaviour, psychology of all sorts, therapy, and many others. The effectiveness of executive coaching is difficult to evaluate as there are knotty methodological conundrums to resolve. It is not a drug therapy or surgical procedure where randomized control trials are relatively easy to organize. Most practitioners settle for the *balance of probabilities* approach used in civil law rather than the absolute proof demanded in a criminal case. Passmore and Fillery-Travis provide a meta-analysis of the current evidence.[3]

## The psychology underpinning coaching

Social psychologists can now look back on a century of research answering questions such as: what motivates people to try harder at work? What gets in the way of change and how can you overcome resistance? What difference does it make to performance when people can articulate their goals? What style of leadership gets the best long-term results?

Motivation is one of the most studied subjects in psychology because so many people have a stake in knowing the answers. If you run a commercial operation you will want to know how to increase output and profit without raising your costs, and you will also know that the answer will depend on people working hard *without being told*, so the most critical question is: how do you do that? If you are a performance director or head coach in a sport where international competition matters and where there is glory and money at stake, you will want to know how to encourage your athletes to reach their peak performance.

Similarly, if you are a clinician with an interest in working with patients more effectively, you will want to know how to create greater openness to new ideas, how to reduce resistance and how to make your expertise available to patients. Fortunately, the same principles apply here as they do in other areas where change and improvement are the issues.

## The power of choice

Coaching is a lot more than just a 'technique' that you switch on and off. It is a radical and all-encompassing new set of assumptions about people.

When you adopt a coaching approach, you believe that human beings have the power of choice. Uniquely among mammals, we have consciousness, we can remember the past, examine our own motivation, imagine the future and use language to express ourselves. As a coach, you believe that whatever life throws at us, we have the power of choice in how we respond. There is always that nanosecond between stimulus and response, and in it we choose how we react, though this may happen so quickly that we can be unaware of it. While remaining respectful and empathetic, the true coach will not go along with ideas such as 'I can't help it', 'He made me do it', 'This is just how I am' or 'It's all because X or Y happened to me in childhood'. What all these statements do is to put the responsibility on to some other person or outside agency. When we do this we take on a victim identity, experience feelings of powerlessness and potentially of depression because we have refused to take responsibility for ourselves. No one can 'make' us happy or unhappy. Similarly, many people are unaware that when they say they can do 'nothing', 'doing nothing' is in itself a choice.

This idea has never been better expressed than by Viktor Frankl, a Jewish neurologist, psychiatrist and Holocaust survivor. In one of the most influential books of the twentieth century, *Man's Search for Meaning*,[4] first published in 1946, Frankl calmly described his experience at Auschwitz where he was deprived of everything that most of us would consider essential for happiness: physical safety, food, clothing, warmth, family, health, profession. The book has sold more than 10 million copies in 25 languages. In a much-quoted passage he wrote:

> in the final analysis it becomes clear that the sort of person the prisoner became was the result of an inner decision, not the result of camp influences alone. Fundamentally therefore, any man can, even under such circumstances, decide what shall become of him, mentally and spiritually. He may retain his human dignity, even in a concentration camp.

At the lowest point of his life in the terrible brutalities of the camp, Frankl had a vision where he saw himself writing, teaching and lecturing about the experience after the war. His sense of purpose sustained him. He founded a successful school of psychotherapy, lived into his nineties and his Institute is still going strong today.

A good way of testing the proposition that we always make our own choices is to think of something that you believe you 'have' to do and then to examine the feelings this creates. Now rephrase the statement as 'I have chosen to…' and consider the difference it makes.

When clinicians apply this principle, they can be astonished at the transformation it makes to their attitudes to patients:

> At first I found it hard to see that this 'choice' principle was true as I suppose I had mentally endorsed the idea that we were entirely driven by our emotional storms. But by chance this week I had a good example. I saw two patients with early-onset Parkinson's, both in their mid-forties, young families, successful careers, prognosis very similar. One alarmed me with his despair, described

himself as being 'in pieces', definitely suicidal ideation. The other has already joined a self-help group; he is tweeting and blogging with optimism, humour and grace. I see now that I have to start in a totally different place with both of them. (Family physician)

Simple illustration: how differently patients respond to exactly the same stimuli, e.g. nervousness about having local anaesthesia. You can have four patients, same ages, same backgrounds, same problems and they are everywhere along the spectrum from quaking with fear to total insouciance. Clearly this is a choice. It's made me think quite differently about how I approach them. (Dentist)

Accepting the power of choice implies an optimistic view of human beings, far more optimistic than many clinicians have traditionally endorsed. When you wholeheartedly accept this principle, it results in a radically different way of treating patients. It means abandoning a parent–child model, realizing that by trying to 'rescue' patients you are undermining and patronizing them and thus depriving them of the chance to take control of their own health.

The traditional approach to problem-solving is to put the emphasis on the problem. Think for a moment about something that is worrying you and write down brief answers to these questions:

- What is this problem?
- What are the symptoms?
- What other things like this have gone wrong in your life?
- Whose fault is it?
- Why are you stuck?
- What will happen if you do not find the answer?

The chances are that this will be an instantly mood-lowering experience. The word *problem*, with all its negative associations of blame and disaster, begins a downward spiral of hopelessness.

Coaching puts the emphasis on solutions. Try looking at the same problem by answering these questions, noting that these questions avoid using the word *problem* at all:

- What's the issue?
- Who/what is involved?

- If you imagine yourself at your most resourceful, what would you say to yourself?
- When you have faced this kind of issue before, what has worked?
- If you imagine that this issue has been resolved, what would be happening?
- What might you try as a first step to a solution?

These questions convey the belief that you could find an answer that will work for you. The mood they create is normally quite different.

## Emotion is more powerful than logic and facts

Training as a clinician equips you with knowledge. The whole point of your role is that you know substantially more than your patients do. Unfortunately, until comparatively recently most of this training assumed that all that had to happen was for knowledge to pass seamlessly and painlessly from clinician to patient: tick, job done! But information is not a commodity. To be absorbed and accepted, it needs to fit with basic human needs and these are all about emotion, not logic.

Neuroscience has demonstrated beyond doubt that human beings are driven by emotion,[5] even though we flatter ourselves by naming our species *Homo sapiens*, meaning wise man, on the assumption that the pre-frontal cortex, greater in humans than in any other mammal, gives us the superior thinking capacity of logic and reason. Indeed it does – but in evolutionary terms the limbic system, the emotional centre of the brain, is older and a great deal more powerful. All our decisions are made here, out of conscious awareness, and justified with rationality later.

Emotion will always be dominant in any human exchange, and the more important that exchange is, the more it will matter to understand how to manage it to get the best result.

## What all human beings need

Twentieth- and twenty-first-century social psychology has offered many helpful frameworks for understanding what all human beings need emotionally, regardless of culture, nationality or race. Many of these frameworks are similar. One of the best-researched and most convincing is *self-determination theory*,[6] developed by Edward Deci and Richard Ryan. Their proposition is that for psychological health, all human beings need three elements (Figure 2.1):

*Autonomy* – being able to make our own decisions, feeling that we are in charge of our own lives.

*Competence* – having skills that we can use and develop.

*Relatedness* – feeling respected by and connected to other people; being liked, being accepted for who we really are.

When we have these we feel able to control our own destiny, and when we feel we can control our own destiny we are more likely to feel happy and fulfilled.

This has major implications for anyone whose job involves one-to-one influencing, including clinicians. Respecting patient *autonomy* means acting in ways that value their right to make their own decisions about their health. Encouraging *competence* means offering chances to enhance the skills involved in managing their conditions, whether this is showing a young patient with asthma how to use an inhaler confidently or engaging a 60-year-old in follow-up DIY physiotherapy that can be done at home. *Relatedness* underpins it all: connecting with patients at the emotional level where they feel welcomed, liked and accepted. These three requirements are the essential conditions which need to be in place for a coaching approach to work. So a doctor who consciously allows the patient to tell the essentials of their story before interrupting to give an immediate diagnosis is honouring the need for autonomy. A community nurse who shows a patient how to apply a dressing themselves is assuming the patient's competence. A hospital consultant creates relatedness when he tells the patient his name, avoids sitting behind a big desk and asks the patient what name they would like used in the consultation.

**Figure 2.1** Essential human needs

# Why 'telling' does not work

Motivation has been extensively researched in the copious literature on management because every boss has an interest in finding out what will make people willing workers. Frederic Laloux's book *Reinventing Organizations*[7] offers another radical slant on this subject, suggesting that most of what we take for granted in management is unnecessary and positively harmful. The conclusions of research are stark: telling and directing is useful in an emergency and can get short-term compliance especially if it is backed up by fear of reprisals; but it never gets commitment, even in the short term, and in the longer term it creates every kind of resistance on a spectrum from subtle undermining to outright sabotage.

When another human being insists on telling, ordering and directing, even it if is done courteously, our typical response is to resist. In terms of neuroscience, the amygdalae in the brain experience it as an attack, so our higher thinking processes shut down. We may fight back with arguing or physical resistance, or else we feel undermined and childlike. Attention goes to proving the other person wrong: 'yes but' is often the immediate response (Figure 2.2).

This will be true even when the person doing the telling is someone we respect. What will typically happen is that we nod politely, so resistance may not be visible. But inside we may feel disappointed – with ourselves for not speaking up, or with the other person for not listening. Or we may feel angry that the other person made such unwarranted assumptions about us when a few questions might have revealed our real worries and concerns.

## We believe what we hear ourselves say

The coaching approach is based on evidence that we believe what we hear ourselves say. When we make our own choices we take ownership of them, we are self-motivated, feel empowered, offer our own ideas and solutions and are far more likely to put them into action (Figure 2.3).

When encouraged to think for ourselves in response to challenging questions sympathetically put, it becomes more difficult to go on droning through the same old opinions. The right questions dismantle

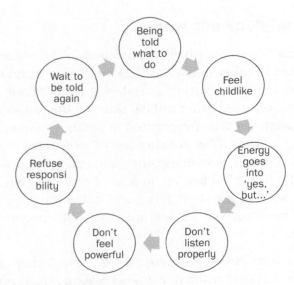

**Figure 2.2** Insistence creates resistance

resistance and uncover a different and better quality of data. A coaching approach to health assumes that because the patient is the one who will implement decisions and live with the results, the art for the clinician is in asking the right questions and offering information in the right way, rather than in telling people what to do.

## Defining health coaching

Health coaching is the art of facilitating the patient's active participation in managing their own health. Coaching raises self-awareness and identifies choices. Through using a coaching approach, patients are able to find their own solutions to enhancing health-related quality of life.

### Six principles of health coaching

Our approach is based on six foundation principles adapted from Jenny Rogers's book *Coaching Skills: A Handbook*:[8]

1. Patients are resourceful.
2. The practitioner's role is to move from expert to enabler.
3. We take a whole-life approach because the patient's health will be affected by everything else that is going on in their life.

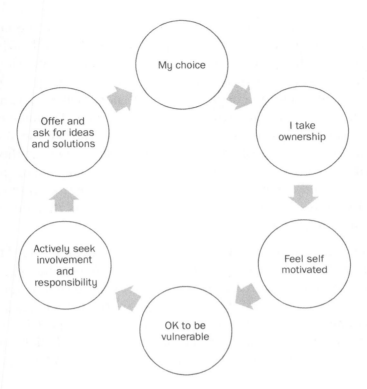

**Figure 2.3** Choice creates empowerment

4. The patient brings the agenda for the consultation.
5. Practitioner and patient are equals in the consultation.
6. Coaching is about change and action.

These principles may seem easy enough to endorse when read flatly in a list, but their collective impact does imply a profound difference in the clinician–patient relationship from the one that is so often the default. The principles imply that patients have the capacity to be resourceful, even when they seem passive or anxious. The principles acknowledge that the patient is the one who is responsible for their health, that they know themselves better than any clinician can, and that it is the patient who lives with the consequences of health decisions, so patients do not need clinicians to rescue, reform them or tell them what to do. It is for this reason that the practitioner's role moves from an emphasis on being an expert to an emphasis on being an enabler and facilitator.

Taking a whole-life approach means that it is essential to enquire into what else is happening for the patient along with whatever their health issue is, because the other issues in their life will have the power to enhance or hinder whatever is going on with their health. When you accept that it is the patient who brings the agenda you are honouring their uniqueness and their need for autonomy. Assuming that you are equals in the consultation implies mutual respect, listening as much as talking and being prepared to do what therapists call 'dancing in the moment', spontaneously sharing control for the flow of the conversation rather than having preconceived ideas about where it should go. Honouring the principle of change means that the expected result of the conversation is that something will change for the better. If the patient does not wish to change, or cannot for some reason, then coaching is not the right approach.

The mindset of the clinician who uses coaching is characterized by curiosity, neutrality and warmth. The curiosity is about how the patient presents their issues, the words they are using to describe it, the things that are being said and not said. The neutrality is about listening attentively to the patient and giving them as much headspace as possible without feeling the need to categorize or intrude with your own beliefs and prejudices. The warmth is about demonstrating empathy and acceptance.

## What's different in health coaching?

Many clinicians already have some familiarity with motivational interviewing, counselling or therapy, all of which have had major influence on coaching for health, but they are still significantly different in a number of ways.

### Motivational interviewing and health coaching

Public health professionals have been faced with many substantial challenges over the last decades: the AIDS epidemic, the disastrous consequences on human health of smoking, the stark increases in obesity, the rapid rise in the numbers of people with diabetes. It quickly became clear that just giving people leaflets or frightening them with television advertising did not change behaviour and that something radically different was needed.

*Motivational interviewing* (MI) originated from work in the 1970s and 1980s with people struggling with substance misuse. It is still the approach used most frequently and effectively with people who want to stop smoking, moderate their drinking or come off addictive drugs. The core of MI is practitioner recognition that giving up an addiction usually involves ambivalence. For instance, on the one hand the smoker recognizes that smoking damages their health, on the other, they may not be perfectly ready to stop right now. MI works through collaboration, through drawing out the person's own ideas about how to stop and by emphasizing their autonomy. The aim is to create trust, offer encouragement, side-step advice-giving and recognize that the only person who can accomplish change is the individual. MI practitioners learn to avoid behaving as authority figures. They do this through expressing empathy, supporting the client's belief in their capacity to change and 'rolling with resistance' – in other words, accepting that resistance is normal and that the way to dismantle it is to go with it, not to argue or insist. MI practitioners will often say that they are 'guide, not god'. There is an entertaining TEDX talk by Bas Bloem[9] on this theme. One recent definition is that MI is 'a collaborative, person-centred form of guiding to elicit and strengthen motivation to change'.[10]

MI closely resembles coaching in its non-judgemental approach and in its emphasis on empathy and trust in the relationship. As with coaching, practitioners are trained to see it as a state of mind rather than as just a set of techniques. We see MI as having many applications in health coaching and have drawn extensively on the MI literature in our own practice and in this book, but its main value is in tackling ambivalence about behavioural change. In MI the practitioner creates and holds the agenda, which is about the desirability of changing behaviour in a well-defined way, whereas in coaching the patient creates the agenda. The Motivational Interviewing Network of Trainers website[11] is a useful resource with further information and research references on MI.

Health coaching is broader than MI because it will include how to handle conversations about all of these: treatment options, tackling social problems, interpreting test results, managing recovery from surgery, pain management, and many others.

## Therapy and health coaching

There are hundreds of schools of therapy, some of them prone to unseemly squabbling with each other about whose theories are 'best', and at the extremes they may appear to have little in common with each other. There are therapies where intricate delving into the past is an essential part of finding resolution for the client. There are others, notably CBT and those drawing on neuro-linguistic programming (NLP) principles, where the emphasis is much more on the present, the future and on action than on the past or on asking the question 'why?', as in 'why does the patient do this?'. There is therapy that can last many years and there is brief therapy, which is typically just six 50-minute sessions. Whatever the differences between approaches to therapy, without the existence of more than a hundred years of therapy as such a helpful forerunner, including its multiplicity of research, there would, for certain, be no coaching.

What therapy, counselling and coaching have in common is the emphasis on warmth, empathy and creating an alliance between practitioner and client. Both highlight the critical importance of close listening of a kind that few people experience anywhere else. Like coaching, most therapists stress the importance as a client of taking responsibility for your own actions. Both coaching and therapy are about change and take a whole-life approach. In both, emotion is all part of what the practitioner expects to deal with. There are many coaches who can skilfully blend therapy with coaching, and many therapists whose work is coaching in all but name.

Nonetheless, in practice there are substantial differences. The most important is implied in the word itself. The word *therapy* comes from the Greek word meaning 'cure', and it is not chance that as a discipline it was developed by psychiatrists. The underlying model is medical. It is based on an assumption that something is wrong – a *dis-ease*. There is an emphasis on interpretation, diagnosis, treatment and healing. Therapy will tend to be problem-oriented, and therapists deal with entrenched difficulties such as depression, obsessive-compulsive disorder, suicidal thoughts or addictions. Treatment options may include medication as well as 'talking cures'. Although many therapists try hard to avoid imbalances of power between themselves and their clients, in practice the therapist usually assumes more authority in the relationship than the client.

Coaching, by contrast, assumes that people are functioning well, even if they appear to be destabilized by some immediate crisis. There is more stress on creating clear goals for the conversation. It focuses on strengths and on what is going right. There is an assumption that even in the darkest moments there will be some cause for optimism. There is no interpretation, 'treatment' or final diagnosis.

Coaching is future- and solution-oriented, with emphasis on action and accountability – not, note, the parent–child or teacher–pupil kind of accountability, but just an interested, friendly and objective person to report to on how your agreed actions and hopeful experiments are going. Whatever the differences in status, age, education, income, profession, for purposes of the conversation, coach and client are equals.

While coaching is not therapy, many coaches have trained in NLP or CBT, both of which are used in mainstream healthcare settings and share similar mindsets to coaching. These include the principle that the client is resourceful and that the practitioner's role is to facilitate the client in tapping into that resourcefulness. Both fields have much of value to offer the practising coach through detailed exploration of the way our behaviour is affected by how we think and feel and by the notion that our perception of experiences has a structure as well as content. This exploration has led to the development of sophisticated approaches and techniques[12,13] on which coaches can draw to enhance their work. Another form of therapy is based on transactional analysis (TA)[14,15] which examines patterns of interaction between people. The principles of TA are highly applicable in coaching and we have referred to them at various points in this book.

## Consultation skills and coaching

Consultation skills are taught on all clinician qualifying courses, and you may be wondering how coaching is different. Apart from the differences we have already described, one critical difference is in the attention paid to language. Dr John Launer,[16] Associate Dean for Faculty Development at Health Education England, puts it like this:

> The vast majority of doctors in most specialties never once sit down to consider systematically the words and phrases they use when conversing with patients, or the tone and manner in which they deliver them ... There is an interesting contrast here between medical doctors and psychological therapists or counsellors ... They approach each consultation with the assumption that the acts of talking and listening will bring about change as a matter of course. ... Therapists learn precise micro-skills that make the conversational skills of many doctors seem crude by comparison. Their training enables them to pick up exact words, hesitations, nuances of tone, or gestures of hands and body and to be able to

follow these through with sensitive questions, or if appropriate, with silence.

In our own practice we have seen how much difference it can make to become profoundly alert to nuances of language. For instance, we will notice when people use generalizations such as 'always' or 'everyone', as in 'Everyone is always so unpleasant to me'. We will notice abstract words such as 'stress' to which the patient may have given some fleeting emphasis, so fleeting that you might miss it. But these abstract words have absolutely no meaning without a behavioural definition. It can transform a consultation to notice the abstract word and to ask the patient to say more about what it means to them, for instance, 'When you say you feel *stressed*, how does feeling stressed actually affect you?'.

Coaching involves a genuinely two-way exchange. In the deepest of ways it is unlike even some of the most enlightened of twentieth-century models of 'patient-centred consultation', most of which still imply that the clinician's role is to be the detective on behalf of the patient, for instance to wheedle out of the patient what their 'hidden' agenda is, assuming that this is a single fixed item. The coaching approach, in contrast, invites the patient to set and make explicit their own agenda from the outset, enabling them to take ownership of this.

Coaching assumes that the patient will affect the clinician just as the clinician affects the patient. It assumes that the conversation is unpredictable because it may contain unexpected twists and turns. It assumes that the patient may have more than one 'agenda' and that there is a whole-life context that will be affecting what the patient's concerns are and what they do with any information that the clinician offers them. Coaching may involve a clinician asking questions which open him or her to discomfort because they focus directly on the relationship, questions which would have been unthinkable in the past, such as 'I'm wondering what you're making of our consultations – what are you getting out of them?'

## The benefits of coaching

As enthusiasts for the coaching approach we are aware of the need to avoid making too many claims for its benefits. However, we do believe these benefits to be substantial.

One benefit to patients is the likelihood of greatly improved communication with their clinicians. Complaints, for instance about communication, have hugely increased,[17] whether this is about doctors who are alleged not to have listened, who use language that the patient cannot understand or who appear standoffish and rude. Good communication of the kind that is involved in coaching is fundamental to good care. Another patient benefit is that a coaching approach encourages and promotes the idea that people can prioritize their health and take responsibility for it without being so dependent on clinical opinion. Patients are likely to feel more confident, more in control and more willing to engage with clinical management plans.

In discussing how using coaching is also good for the clinician, the people we have trained consistently report greater satisfaction with their work, reduced stress, and fewer patients who appear to be impossible to help. These clinicians are able to distinguish the occasions when it is essential to take responsibility for the patient and the majority when it is not – and releasing yourself from inappropriate responsibility immediately reduces stress. Such clinicians are also far less likely to be the focus of complaints. If you deal with patients with long-term conditions or 'grey area' conditions like chronic fatigue, fibromyalgia and medically unexplained pain, it is easy to feel hopeless and inadequate. Coaching puts an emphasis on seeing problems in different ways and on looking for what works as well as what is failing, so it can create hope on both sides where other interventions have not, as these two primary care physicians report:

> I no longer have 'difficult' patients since I started using a coaching approach, I feel more in control of the consultation, more aware that I can't do everything and a lot less stressed.

> Previously I often ended the day feeling as helpless as many of my patients. It's forced me to examine a lot of my assumptions about what patients could and couldn't do or understand. It feels like a shared responsibility, whereas previously it felt like it was all down to me.

The benefits are not limited to patients and clinicians operating solo. Coaching has the potential to reduce inappropriate prescribing and unnecessary repeat consultations and emergency admissions to hospital, saving time and money.[18] Since coaching is essentially about excellence in communication, we hear constantly from our course participants that they have been able to use their coaching skills in a wide range of other settings, including with their families, with other clinicians and within their teams. This is going to matter more and more when the emphasis is increasingly on integrated care. People with training responsibilities report being able to have more effective conversations with their trainees; people whose work brings them into constant contact with managers say that they are able to work far more collaboratively than in the past, where relationships have sometimes been tense. All of this is good for organizations, smoothing the way its systems work and thus ultimately improving patient safety and care.

## What's the evidence that it works?

There is a growing body of international evidence, mainly originating from the USA and more recently the UK, pointing specifically to the benefits of health coaching approaches, including its use in diabetes, asthma, smoking cessation, obesity, cardiovascular disease, mental health and medication adherence. The Evidence Centre[18] has published a review of the empirical evidence relating to health coaching. The review highlights that the methodology used in studies of the effectiveness of health coaching is often not robust and that there is limited research on long-term effects. The studies are difficult to compare with each other for a host of reasons, including large variations in the definitions of health coaching, methods of delivery – for example, whether it was face-to-face or done by telephone – types of professional delivering the coaching, and also variations in patient populations and settings. There are also inconsistencies in the competencies used and in the level of training and experience of the healthcare professionals providing health coaching approaches.

### Benefits to patients

The research community has been taking steps to begin addressing these gaps and issues. The findings from some recent and ongoing studies are encouraging. For example, 800 healthcare professionals drawn from 31 organizations across the East of England were trained in health coaching skills from April 2013 to October 2014. An interim report[19] has reported patient and financial benefits which included 'reduced tests and activity resulting from more effective consultations; improved health behaviours; improved patient motivation to self-care; patients setting self-determined goals; improved medication compliance; developing shared responsibility and improved health'. Key learning for clinicians involved 'developing a mindset shift from expert to enabler, sharing responsibility with patients and adopting a more flexible consultation style'. The website is updated frequently as further reports become available. The evaluation of a Department of Health-funded pilot run by the London Deanery[20] also reported shifts in clinicians' mindset, attitude and confidence in supporting people with long-term conditions following training in health coaching skills, with patients reporting benefits including weight loss, smoking cessation and adherence to medications. Duke Integrative Medicine,[21] based in the USA, is leading research, including randomized controlled clinical trials, on health coaching for long-term conditions such as diabetes and cardiovascular disease.

## Benefits to clinicians

The evidence on benefits to clinicians is still emerging, but our own impression is that the benefits to clinicians are as powerful as they are to patients. This is supported by work that has investigated the relationship between clinician communication behaviour, patient satisfaction ratings and clinician stress. For instance, in one study,[22] the more a clinician adopted a verbally dominant style with minimal emphasis on creating rapport, the less likely their patients were to feel satisfied with their treatment and the more likely these clinicians were to report burnout and emotional exhaustion. The same results have been found in the teaching profession, where research[23] has suggested that teachers who do not value personal relationships with their students and who hold demanding, authoritarian attitudes experience significantly more stress.

The likely reason is the phenomenon we have described earlier in this chapter, that the more you attempt to control, the greater the resistance you create and the more extra energy it takes to try to stay on top, generating an ever increasing spiral of pointless effort. This behaviour is common in organizations where there is a hierarchy – which is to say, most organizations. The distinguished writer on management, Stephen Covey, puts it like this in his book *The 8th Habit: From Effectiveness to Greatness:*[24]

The more a manager controls, the more he/she evokes behaviors that necessitate greater control or managing. The co-dependent cult that develops is eventually institutionalized to the point where no one takes responsibility. They disempower themselves by believing that others must change before their own circumstances improve.

Not many people are brave enough even to recognize it [their co-dependency] in themselves. Whenever they hear the idea they instinctively look *outside* themselves.

## Why coaching works

Coaching works because it assumes that the patient is resourceful and taps into that resourcefulness. By assuming that the patient is the one who knows themselves best and who must live with the results of any treatment, it puts a premium on empathy, on careful listening and on respect for patient choices, even when such choices seem 'unwise' to the clinician. By doing this it increases the chances that the most important problems will be dealt with swiftly, thus reducing attendance at family practice sessions and outpatient clinics. Treating patients as equals and genuine partners in the management of their health is more likely to reduce inappropriate prescribing or unnecessary and ineffectual treatments of all kinds.

All clinical management is about change. As patients, we want something to be different: to feel less depressed, to have better pain management, to be reassured, to choose the right option for surgery, to get the correct medication for whatever is wrong. But change is not a simple process. We may want the eventual outcomes of the change and yet resist the path to getting there. To help patients make beneficial change it is essential to understand why as patients we may not accept the information we are given, why we may resist being given advice – and as a clinician to know what to do instead, all topics that we explore in the chapters that follow.

## Summary

Coaching is underpinned by research showing that human beings function best when we make and live with the results of our own decisions.

It suggests that advice-giving, the traditional approach of clinicians, unless done very skilfully, is often counterproductive because it compromises the universal human needs for autonomy, feeling competent and relating authentically to others. Motivational interviewing, therapy and executive coaching have all helped form our current understanding of how health coaching can improve the quality of communication with patients, increase levels of patient safety, reduce clinician stress, reduce inappropriate prescribing, with all of this saving time and costs as well as equipping clinicians with skills that are valuable in every part of their lives.

# References

1. Seligman, M. *Authentic happiness.* https://www.authentichappiness.sas.upenn.edu/ (accessed 3 November 2014).
2. Whitmore, J. *Coaching for Performance.* London: Nicholas Brealey; 1992.
3. Passmore, J. and Fillery-Travis, A. A critical review of executive coaching research: A decade of progress and what's to come. *Coaching: An International Journal of Theory, Practice & Research* 2011; 4(2), 70–88.
4. Frankl, V. *Man's Search for Meaning.* Boston: Beacon Press; 1984.
5. Coricelli, G., Dolan, R.J. and Sirigu, A. Brain, emotion and decision making: the paradigmatic example of regret. *Trends in Cognitive Sciences* 2007; 11(6): 258–265.
6. Ryan, R.M. and Deci, E.L. Self-determination theory and the facilitation of intrinsic motivation, social development and wellbeing. *American Psychologist* 2000; 55(1): 68–76.
7. Laloux, F. *Reinventing Organizations.* Brussels: Nelson Parker; 2014.
8. Rogers, J. *Coaching Skills: A Handbook* (3rd edition). Maidenhead: Open University Press; 2012.
9. Bloem, B. *From God to Guide.* https://www.youtube.com/watch?v=LnDWt10Maf8 (accessed 23 February 2015).
10. Miller, W.R. and Rollnick, S. Ten things that motivational interviewing is not. *Behavioural and Cognitive Psychotherapy* 2009; 37: 129–140.
11. MINT. *Motivational Interviewing.* http://motivationalinterviewing.org/?reqp=1&reqr= (accessed 23 February 2015).
12. Thomson, G. and Khan, K. *Magic in Practice: Introducing Medical NLP – The Art and Science of Language in Healing and Health* (2nd edition). London: Hammersmith Health Books; 2015.
13. David, L. *Using CBT in General Practice: The 10 Minute Consultation.* Banbury: Scion Publishing; 2006.
14. Berne, E. *Games People Play: The Psychology of Human Relationships.* London: Penguin; 2010.
15. Stewart, I. and Joines, V. *TA Today: A New Introduction to Transactional Analysis.* (2nd edition). Chapel Hill, NC: Lifespace Publishing; 2012.

16. Launer, J. Conversations inviting change. *Postgraduate Medical Journal* 2008; 84: 4–5.
17. Levinson, W., Roter, D.L., Mullooly, J.P., Dull, V.T. and Frankel, R.M. Physician-patient communication. The relationship with malpractice claims among primary care physicians and surgeons. *Journal of the American Medical Association* 1997; 277: 553–559.
18. The Evidence Centre. *Does Health Coaching Work? Summary of key themes from a rapid review of empirical evidence.* https://www.eoeleadership.nhs.uk/sites/default/files/Does%20health%20coaching%20work%20-%20summary.pdf (accessed 7 June 2015).
19. Health Education East of England. *Health Coaching Interim Progress Report.* https://eoeleadership.hee.nhs.uk/sites/default/files/1404813191_LmkH_health_coaching_interim_progress_report.pdf (accessed 7 June 2015).
20. London Deanery. *Training GP Trainees in Health Coaching: Feasibility and Impacts.* https://www.networks.nhs.uk/nhs-networks/sha-shared-decision-making-and-information-giving/documents/Impact%20of%20health%20coaching%20-%20London%20Deanery.pdf (accessed 20 November 2014).
21. Duke Integrative Medicine. *Research.* http://www.dukeintegrativemedicine.org/research (accessed 29 December 2014).
22. Ratanawongsa, N., Korthuis, P.T., Saha, S., Roter, D., Moore, R.D., Sharp, V.L. and Beach, M.C. Clinician stress and patient–clinician communication in HIV care. *Journal of General Internal Medicine* 2012; 27(12): 1635–1642.
23. Larrivee, B. *Cultivating Teacher Renewal: Guarding against Stress and Burnout.* Lanham, MD: Rowman & Littlefield Education; 2012.
24. Covey, S.R. *The 8th Habit: From Effectiveness to Greatness.* New York: Simon & Schuster; 2006.

# 3 CORE SKILLS OF THE CLINICIAN-COACH

In this chapter we introduce the core skills of coaching. You may have already acquired many of them, in which case our aim is to reconnect you with their importance in creating a powerful clinical consultation where patient and clinician are partners.

Clinical training always includes some basic instruction in communication, including how to create rapport, listen, take a case history and ask questions. Health systems claim that they want to support individuals in promoting and managing their own health. In practice, in twenty-first-century clinical practice, the principles of how to put the patient at the centre of their own care are often compromised or forgotten. Patients may still experience their clinicians as disconnected, uninterested and hard to interrupt. Doing a Google search of "my doctor doesn't listen to me" will reveal find multiple patient blog sites and conversation forums which discuss this common lament.

Social media and the rise of the internet have highlighted this issue with campaigns such as Kate Granger's #HelloMyNameIs.[1] Kate Granger, a young doctor with a rare and incurable form of soft tissue cancer which spread to her liver and bones, was shocked at her own experience as a patient. She wrote prolifically and movingly about her sense of becoming a case rather than an individual, suggesting the small, simple steps that healthcare providers can take to humanize clinical encounters. She felt that the dehumanizing process started when so many of the clinicians providing her care neglected the simple courtesy of introducing themselves:[2]

> One of the starkest observations...was the absence of introductions from the staff delivering my care. It wasn't just the occasional

slip but something that seemed to permeate through the professional groups and support staff. When someone did offer a friendly introduction, however, it made all the difference. It began a relationship, helped to put me at ease relieving my anxieties and humanized what can in many circumstances be an extremely dehumanizing experience. When introductions were missing, I was left wondering who the person was and feeling that I was just another body with a disease in a hospital bed...I also believe it is the first rung on the ladder to providing compassionate care by establishing a human connection and building trust with a person.

It soon became clear that my experience was not a unique one, with scores of other patients and carers taking the opportunity to tell me about their dislike of absent introductions, and what a huge impact a welcoming introduction can make to the confidence they had in their healthcare team.

The ingenuity of this idea is its simplicity. It costs nothing and takes only seconds, but it improves patient experience. It is the first step to discovering what matters to that individual and to putting their concerns first. ... As a patient, I believe that it is the little things like this that make the biggest difference.

Dr Granger began a campaign on Twitter using the hashtag #HelloMyNameIs. The campaign spread rapidly to the point where it has become embedded in the values and policy of many healthcare organizations, but it is still shocking that such a campaign was and is necessary.

Many factors compromise the quality of clinical consultations. In busy clinical settings, healthcare providers are often distracted, overloaded with work, time-poor and, in around a quarter of cases, suffering from 'burnout',[3] a collection of mental symptoms that are the result of unrelenting stress. When this happens, you will be aware that you function in what feels like survival mode, trying to get through each case as quickly as possible, making it unlikely that you will engage warmly and individually with each patient.

Despite communication skills training now being part of every curriculum, clinical practice may still be imbued with paternalism, especially where the clinician has been cast in the role of expert. Advice-giving may still be a central part of the medical consultation, a style that is modelled repeatedly to medical and nursing students during their apprenticeship.

This is matched by learning that our own role when we are patients is to accept the maxim that 'clinicians know best'. This is inculcated in all of us from an early age, whatever our standing in society and level of education, and even today, despite the rise of patient advocacy and easy access to information via the Internet, many of us have not been empowered to expect and ask for more. Putting coaching skills at the heart of the consultation represents a fundamental shift away from this mindset. Instead it is about a relationship of equals in which the clinician-coach asks powerful questions to enhance the patient's belief that they can take charge of their own health.

Dr Atul Gawande, the American surgeon and writer (see also pages 10, 116 and 199) explores this in relation to dying patients in his book, *Being Mortal: What Really Matters in the End*:[4]

> A few years ago, I got a late night page: Jewel Douglass, a 72-year-old patient of mine receiving chemotherapy for metastatic ovarian cancer, was back in the hospital, unable to hold food down. For a week, her symptoms had mounted... A scan showed that, despite treatment, her ovarian cancer had multiplied, grown, and partly obstructed her intestine.
>
> But walking into Douglass' hospital room, I'd never have known she was so sick if I hadn't seen the scan. 'Well, look who's here!' she said, as if I'd just arrived at a cocktail party. 'How are you, doctor?'... Here it was, 11 at night, she couldn't hold down an ounce of water, and she still had her lipstick on, her silver hair was brushed straight, and she was insisting on making introductions.
>
> Her oncologist and I had a menu of options....This is the moment when I would normally have reviewed the pros and cons. But we are only gradually learning in the medical profession that this is not what we need to do. The options overwhelmed her... So I stepped back and asked her a few questions ... hoping to better help both of us know what to do: What were her biggest fears and concerns? What goals were most important to her? What trade-offs was she willing to make?

Not all can answer such questions, but she did. She said she wanted to be without pain, nausea, or vomiting. She wanted to eat. Most of all, she wanted to get back on her feet. Her biggest fear was that she wouldn't be able to return home and be with the people she loved.

I asked what sacrifices she was willing to endure now for the possibility of more time later...Uppermost in her mind was a wedding that weekend that she was desperate not to miss. She was supposed to be a bridesmaid. She was willing to do anything to make it, she said.

Suddenly, with just a few simple questions, I had some guidance about her priorities. So we made a plan to see if we could meet them.

## Creating the right first impression

The old saying has it that you never have a second chance to create a first impression. Rapport can be destroyed in seconds if this goes wrong. In this example, the patient has been referred to a large hospital with a non-healing lesion on his scalp:

A cross-looking man emerges and calls my name. Doesn't tell me his so he has never heard of #HelloMyNameIs. I briefly glimpse from the plaque on the door that it is Dr X. Complains grumpily that I don't have the 'right' paperwork. He looks at the lesion for about 3 seconds. Grunts. I have to ask for the diagnosis.

'I think it's a squamous cell carcinoma and it needs to come out asap, ideally today.'

No explanation for this diagnosis was offered. Instead he rushes off looking annoyed, muttering about the terrible hospital systems and how inefficient everything is.

A nice senior nurse appears, introduces herself pleasantly so she has heard of #HelloMyNameIs and leads me to the treatment room and unhurriedly invites and answers my questions. She recognizes that any diagnosis with the word 'cancer' in it has the power to alarm and she is reassuring without being over-reassuring. Dr X returns and scrubs up. It's possible his scowl had abated at this point but if so I couldn't see as I was lying on my side away from him.

Ten painless minutes later my scalp has several neat stitches. He doesn't say goodbye and there is no chance to ask questions.

This patient's husband has just had a scan after further symptoms which suggest that his liver cancer has returned:

We were taken into a room where the surgeon had been joined by four people. None was introduced and there was no explanation then or later of why they were there. Throughout the whole encounter, the surgeon repeatedly glanced at the clock, despite having to give us the grim news that Michael's scan had shown that he had new secondaries in his liver and that more surgery would be needed. I insisted on asking questions but I could see that this was unwelcome and the surgeon looked meaningfully at the clock again. We were reeling from the bad news. It was all so very badly handled.

The doctor never looked at me once during the 6 minutes I was there. His eyes remained firmly on his computer screen including the moments when I entered and left the room.

## Building rapport

Nothing creative can happen in a clinical consultation without rapport. It is rapport that allows a patient to express their concerns honestly and to take risks in disclosing what is really going on for them. It is the essence of a good coaching conversation because it sets direction for the rest of the conversation. To a large extent, building rapport is simply an extension of many of the skills that you will already have and use. It is about using observational skills to pay intricate attention to what is happening in the room and to the subtle cues that the patient gives you, verbal and non-verbal. You will do this anyway, but a coaching conversation takes it to the next level. What does that tiny shift in posture mean during the conversation? What was the meaning of the flicker of concern that passed over the patient's face? These skills may seem simple, but they are rare. It is unusual to be offered 100 per cent attention and care by another human being, and it is enormously validating when we do receive it.

What happens if rapport is compromised? The results for you as the clinician and for the patient are profound. The risk for the patient is that their story will not be heard and understood and the conversation may be impoverished as a result. You may miss valuable clues because, as a result of lack of trust and connection, the patient may withhold vital information about their clinical history.

### Rapport checklist

Smile. It's the most fundamental and basic method for communicating goodwill between human beings and goes a long way in building rapport. It puts patients at ease, regardless of the circumstances.

Pay careful attention to where you place yourself in the room, and the height and position of the chairs and desk. Choose chairs of identical design, and avoid having a desk between you.

If you are going to write notes during the consultation, you may want to weigh up the value of capturing detail accurately against the loss of eye contact. Ideally, listen first and write later.

Non-verbal cues are important ways of conveying that you are listening: eye contact, nodding, and making small supportive statements such as 'I see'.

A few simple words can set an anxious patient at ease at the beginning of the consultation. This might take the form of a brief enquiry about their journey to the hospital, surgery or department, or a simple enquiry about their comfort, for example, 'Are you OK for us to begin?'.

We can greatly underestimate the power of touch in clinical consultations. Decide whether it is appropriate for you to shake the patient's hand or not when you first greet them. If you do not, the simple act of helping a patient up from the examination couch by offering a hand or arm may help to build rapport in a non-threatening way.

Pay close attention to the unspoken nuances of the conversation. If you notice the patient looks concerned, frightened, irritated, relieved, then name it and explore it further. By showing the patient you are noticing these subtle cues, you are demonstrating that you hear them and see them.

Avoid carping or grumbling about 'the system' or gossiping and bad-mouthing colleagues. This undermines trust and rapport, and makes patients feel more apprehensive and unsure that they can trust you. What if you treat their information in the same way?

## Putting it into practice

Here is one example[5] of how rapport-building and creating the right first impression can work in practice, written by Dr Grahame Brown a consultant in musculoskeletal disorders:

> My first priority now is to build rapport with the patient in the short time I have with them. Instead of keeping the head down over paperwork till a prospective heartsink patient is seated, then greeting them with a tense smile (as all too many doctors do) I now go into the waiting room to observe in a natural way how they look, how they stand…and whether they exhibit any 'pain behaviours' such as sighing or limping. I shake them warmly by the hand and begin a conversation on our way to the consulting area. 'It's warm today isn't it? Did you find your way here all right?' By the time we are seated, the patient has already agreed with me several times. We are already allies, not adversaries – an essential part of rapport building which is too often skipped over in the traditional medical model. Next, rather than assuming the patient has come to see me about their pain, I ask *them* what they have come to see me about. Even though I will have read their notes, I assume nothing. I ask open ended questions that can give me the most information – the facts which are important to *them*.

## The delicate question of names

Nothing gets our attention quite like the use of our own names. But which name? People staffing telephone helplines, whom we have never met and never will meet, may cheerfully address us by our first name despite not having asked or been given permission. People in service roles, for instance waiting staff, will frequently introduce themselves by their first names perhaps emphasizing that they are there to do our bidding. Depending on which country or part of which country you live in, you may be routinely addressed with old-fashioned courtesy as Sir or Ma'am. Electronic message boards, the ones whose function is to tell waiting patients that they are next, frequently use first name and second name with no formal titles: 'First Name + Second Name Go to Room 2'. We know of many patients who say that this strikes them as rude and intrusive.

As clinician and patient get closer in their mutual quest for the continuing good health of the patient, what is the correct naming protocol? If rapport and equality are desirable, should both sides use first names?

This is a more complex question that it looks:

> The friendly surgeon who treated me always addressed me by my first name, even though he had never asked if he could. By chance I met him at a party and introduced him to my companion as 'Professor X'. He smiled and said, 'Oh please, it's [first name + last name].' Was this a hint that at my next follow-up I should use his first name? I didn't think so! At the next appointment I just took refuge in a neutral 'you'. I noticed that his students called him 'Prof'.

> I was appalled to be called by my first name by a young doctor at least thirty years my junior. Despite being clad in the usual terrible non-meeting hospital gown I said, 'Mrs X to you my lad'. He looked surprised and had the grace to blush.

It can be just as tricky for the clinician:

> I don't want to be in social relationships with my patients. In a typical week, I will be doing all sorts of intimate physical examinations of men and women of all ages, listening to patients' deepest worries and secrets, breaking bad, life-changing news, dealing with all manner of intense patient emotions, and all the while needing to remain objective and keep a distance in order to do the job effectively and not burn out. Keeping things on a professional level seems somehow to legitimize and normalize what goes on in the consulting room.

> I introduced myself to one patient, about the same age as me, as 'Hello, my name is Mike [+ surname]. I'm a doctor and one of the orthopaedic team. I'll be looking after you during your stay'. The patient gave me a huge grin, stretched out his hand and said, 'Oh, hi Mike, nice to meet you'. This felt so wrong – and I didn't know what to do! I felt like saying, 'No, we're not at a wedding or some pop concert and I'm not your new best friend.'

Social and professional status governs how we refer to ourselves and others. Using your own or someone else's first name can be a sign that you consider yourself to be an equal or possibly the social inferior of another person. So, for instance, adults refer to children by their first names but expect to have a formal title used by the child. A patient who invites a doctor to use his or her first name may appear to be expressing a desire to be in a more childlike and dependent position – or are they just confident and happy? Professionals who may feel that they are lower down the clinical hierarchy commonly introduce themselves to patients by their first names, while calling the patient by a formal title. This may suggest that the clinician sees him or herself as having lower status than the patient:

> The nurse introduced herself to me as Martina, but she always referred to me as Mr [surname]. I found this a bit false and asked her to call me by my first name.

> The hygienist returned my call about a query I had and said 'Hello Mrs [surname] it's Brian from the dental practice.'

If first names are expected on both sides, it may be an advantage or a handicap:

> It can be difficult as a doctor to be a patient. During my antenatal appointments, the midwife and nurses introduced themselves by first names and called me by my first name. This was intended to create the feeling of being equals, but it felt less professional and somehow less safe in terms of what I felt able to talk to them about.

> I went to the physio for work on my knee and hip. He's youngish, about my own age, introduced himself by his first name and called me by mine. For some reason he had dimmed the lights in the room, plus there was soft music and that and lying down plus my state of undress and the first name stuff somehow introduced a sexual dynamic. I felt very uneasy.

> Junior doctors and medical students in my hospital are expected to call a distinguished senior colleague 'Sir' or 'Professor' (no surname) and expect to be an anonymous 'you' in return. In front of patients, senior doctors will often address a nursing colleague as 'Nurse' (no name) – emphasizing the formality of the role above the individual's status. The intention may be to reassure patients, but does it?

So the choices on both sides are as listed in Table 3.1.

**Table 3.1**   Options for the use of names

| Clinician introduces self as/expects patient to use | Clinician addresses patient by/as |
|---|---|
| Formal title plus surname, no first name | Formal title |
| Role name | Formal title |
| Role name or formal title as above | First name or formal title |
| First name + surname | First name |
| First name | First name |
| Anonymous 'you' | Anonymous 'you' |

There is no evidence that we know of which suggests that trying to create more intimacy through the mutual use of first names improves the quality of the consultation. In other service professions there are different naming customs, so for instance in executive coaching no coach would dream of using anything but first names, however exalted the client.

It is possible to cause great offence by appearing to patronize a patient by using a first name without permission or to appear aloof and uninterested by using their formal title and surname. The answer to the naming conundrum is to think it through carefully. Your choices and the choices of your patients will be affected by age, custom, gender, nationality, culture, professional and social status, the nature of your specialty and what you want to achieve in the consultation. Hiding behind formality on your side but using a patient's first name will create an imbalance of power, but there may be times when this feels right. Sticking to formality on both sides may feel safe as it will emphasize that this is a professional relationship and not a friendship. If in doubt, ask permission and be guided by what the patient says, or negotiate something that feels mutually satisfactory.

## Creating a relationship of equals

A coaching conversation means that you suspend all judgement and accept that despite your expert role and years of experience, in practice you cannot really know what is going on in someone else's life. The patient has to be the expert in the consultation, because they are the expert in their own lives. How would I treat an equal and what would I say to someone if I truly believed that they were entirely capable of making their own decisions?

This sounds so easy but it is more subtle and difficult to master than it looks:

> I had always paid lip service to the idea that the patient and I were equals as I knew that this was how I was 'supposed' to feel as a modern doctor. But it wasn't until I went on the coaching training and started using these techniques myself, that I really began to believe it, and then transforming things started to happen in my consultations.

> It's so hard to turn off judgement. This is especially true when you are experienced and you believe you have seen hundreds of similar patients with similar conditions, but when you do turn it off, I have found that you get surprised because the truth is that no patient is exactly like any other. As a patient myself, would I want to be treated as 'just a case'? No.

As it is impossible to eliminate judgement entirely, it helps to make a point of asking yourself 'What assumptions am I making about this patient or their situation?'. It might be especially important to check out assumptions or judgements when you see a patient who for some reason makes you uncomfortable or irritated:

> My patient was smoking heavily in her home environment as was her partner, and consulting repeatedly with reports that her child had asthma. I noticed my irritation which was about inappropriate use of resources. By being aware of this and getting past it, I was still able to provide a compassionate and useful clinical interaction by asking myself 'What does this judgement tell me about what is going on for the patient – and for me?'.

In these situations it is not about denying or feeling guilty that such judgements exist, but rather about bringing awareness to your consultation so that you can get out of your own way.

## Lessons from transactional analysis

The *drama triangle* is a useful model developed from transactional analysis.[6,7] It describes the roles or 'games' that we can fall into in human interactions, especially when we are under pressure and stress. The roles are shown in Figure 3.1.

The theory suggests that 'players' are acting in some way to get their own unconscious needs met. The drama triangle is a dynamic model because the players constantly shift roles. So when the rescuer tries to rescue, the victim may turn on them, complaining that their rescuing is not helpful enough, thus becoming the persecutor. Or the persecutor, if attacked by the rescuer for bullying, may collapse in self-pity, complaining that they are only doing their best to provide direction and no one appreciates them, thus becoming the victim, making the rescuer now the persecutor. Feeling guilty, the previous victim now tries a little rescuing, comforting the new victim.

**Victim**
Poor me
I'm blameless.
Look after me;
Love me no matter what
I do

**Persecutor**
I'm strong; I
have power

I'm right; I like
control

It's your fault

**Rescuer**
I can help you;

I need to look after
people; I enjoy
dependency

You are helpless; I
know what's best
for you

**Figure 3.1** The drama triangle

The drama triangle is seductive: the players become self-absorbed, unable to think beyond their own needs. The false sense of excitement the game creates distracts them from the real issues and therefore from solving their problems. The pay-off is the short-term reward that this excitement generates and the refuge it seems to supply from dealing with the real underlying issues. There are no winners in the drama triangle. It is about connection – the crisis of the game provides an intensity which should be present in the relationships themselves but that we avoid out of fear.

Many of the clinicians we train have found the drama triangle useful in thinking about roles during a consultation. It can be especially seductive to assume the role of rescuer with some patients, holding them in the victim role, and some clinicians may unconsciously enjoy having someone dependent on them. This does not benefit the patient or you in the long run:

> I work in an area of high deprivation. It's easy to slip into feeling sorry for patients and trying to rescue them and with Mrs D, I did, suggesting that I might be able to help with a referral to social services. I could see that this had not gone down too well but I didn't understand why until she complained about me, alleging that I was trying to get her kids taken away from her. So she started as the victim and I as the rescuer. She then became the persecutor and since I had to defend myself, I became the victim.

As difficult, but rarely talked about even in private, is the reaction to the patient whom you do not like or respect or whom you resent in some way. Here it is easy to fall into the persecutor role and even be tempted to chastise the patient in some way in your role as expert. Next time you feel that a consultation may be derailing or failing to progress, or if you feel drawn to judge or chastise a patient, ask yourself if there is some games-playing going on and if so, what role you have assumed.

## Talking about yourself

Should you talk about yourself? Therapists and counsellors are warned never to do this: their personal lives are off limits, and this is one of the ways that they consider protects them from inappropriate intimacy with clients, allows clients to express themselves freely, as well as preserving mystique and authority. Our own belief is that some extremely judicious sharing may occasionally be right. It humanizes and makes you more approachable – for instance, 'I had the same worry with my own child'. Also, if you have been ill yourself, patients may already know, may be genuinely concerned on your behalf as well as anxious to be reassured that you are fit enough to practise:

> I knew my surgeon had cancer. He's only a young man and I felt sorry. I asked him how he was and he was very frank with me, saying the experience had been 'scary' and that driving anywhere near the hospital where he'd been successfully treated gave him a shiver of anxiety. I was so glad he said this; I felt it put us on a new footing because he was saying he knew himself what it was like to be vulnerable and afraid.

But beware of sharing too much or of prolonging the discussion, or else the patient may feel that you have swapped roles and that they have somehow become the clinician and you the patient.

## Co-creating a goal

This is one of the most profound ways in which the coaching approach and the traditional approach to consultations differ. There is a finite time for any clinical consultation, and your own aims and those of the patient may not always coincide. Having an effective coaching conversation means addressing this possible clash from the outset and co-creating a common purpose for the conversation. This means asking the patient the questions which will get to the heart of what matters to them. Your first question is potentially the most important. An example of a question in the traditional style, in which the clinician sets the agenda, might be:

> We're meeting today to talk about the next round of chemo, and to discuss side effects of your current medication. I hope that's what you were expecting?

In contrast, a clinician using a coaching style says he or she has things to discuss but asks the patient what their agenda is:

> I have a couple of things I would like to cover today which we can come to a minute, but first I want to ask what you want to get out of this conversation. What's on your mind?

Other good opening questions after initial pleasantries will include:

What brings you here today?

What's our agenda for today?

What's going to be the most useful way of using the time we have together for you?

Why does having a goal matter so much? Goals matter because you want the patient to leave the consultation with a feeling of power over their difficulties and that they have a sense of momentum and progress. In the finite time available for any consultation this will only happen if you can create a goal which is meaningful for them. It also helps you as the clinician, as if you jump to conclusions about what the patient wants to achieve from a consultation, you may get it very wrong:

> This was one of those patients who often presented with multiple complex symptoms, who once again presented with pain in her abdomen. I had just done the coaching course and just in time I remembered about setting goals. I had felt powerless and hopeless in the face of yet another medically unexplained symptom until I asked the patient a goal-setting question. It turned out that she was not looking for a diagnosis at all, instead simply wanted the reassurance that the symptom was not caused by serious underlying pathology.

You might also experiment with helping patients to reframe their goals more positively. For example, 'I want to achieve a healthy weight' rather than 'I have to lose weight'; 'I want to live in a smoke-free environment' or 'I want to be a good role model for my children' rather than 'I must give up smoking'.

## Too many goals?

The unusual chance to talk to a non-judgemental person who creates wonderful rapport may produce a torrent of potential goals, each of which may seem as if it is equally important to the patient. The best way to deal with this is openly and at the beginning of the consultation, for instance reminding patients what most will already know all too well, that the consultation time is limited, but to do this in a way which shares responsibility:

All these things sound important but, given that we've got limited time today, which one is the most urgent for you?

Do you feel that all these symptoms are connected, or are they separate?

Could we set some of these aside to discuss at a later appointment?

## Goal-setting in practice

Here are two contrasting ways of starting a consultation with a patient with cancer:

### Clinician sets the agenda

Yvette comes to the hospital for her next oncology appointment to discuss next steps in treatment of her breast cancer. Twenty minutes late, a nurse ushers her in to the consulting room, and the doctor hurries in looking flustered; he does not greet her by name. He sits behind his desk on a large swivel-style leather chair and spends some of the consultation scrolling through files on his computer, trying to find scan results. He cannot find the data. He rolls his eyes complaining to Yvette about the hospital's inefficiency. He tells her that the purpose of the consultation is to discuss the next steps in her treatment. He ends by dictating a letter to her primary care physician while she is in the room, using many medical terms with which she is unfamiliar. She feels unable to ask about them nor to raise any of the many questions that are running through her head. She comments later that 'he seemed distracted and overstretched'.

### Patient sets the agenda

Nicholas has testicular cancer: a stage 1 non-seminoma. He is invited to the hospital to discuss next steps in his treatment. He has already been asked and has requested that his doctor refers to him as 'Nick'. Stewart, the doctor, greets him by name in the waiting room, shakes his hand warmly, smiles and makes eye contact with him. He then leads him into the consulting room and the two of them take a seat in identical chairs set at a 45 degree angle.

Stewart says, 'I have several things on my list to discuss with you, but let's start with your concerns. What do you want to raise today?'

He keeps up his friendly demeanour with Nick, maintains eye contact with him during the conversation, and does not take notes.

Nick hesitates, then says, 'I'm worried about what you said about *surveillance* and *close follow-up* – what if it isn't enough? What if the cancer has already spread?'

'That's your main worry? But perhaps you have others as well?'

Nick nods but says that's the main one – he has others he'd like to raise later.

'OK let's deal with that one first'.

The doctor notices that Nick is speaking quietly and hesitantly during this early part of the consultation, and mirrors this volume in his voice. He also pays careful attention to Nick's body language for clues about how he is feeling.

Having explained the rationale for the treatment plan, Stewart asks, 'How are you feeling about this now?'

Nick's body language has changed. He is sitting in a more upright way and some of the tension has gone from his face. He now feels confident enough to produce a piece of paper with some scribbled further questions. He leaves feeling reassured that he fully understands his options. The doctor, too, feels satisfied with the consultation. He realizes that he had no need to give his prepared speech about why one round of chemotherapy plus medication is desirable in Nick's case because all of this has been amply dealt with by following a patient-led agenda.

## The impact of powerful questions

A coaching conversation is characterized by incisive and powerful questions which get to the heart of the patient's concerns. There is an art in asking the right question. The first tip is to keep it short.

> So taking everything into account and bearing in mind that you have proved intolerant to drug x, and having to keep side effects in mind generally, now that I've talked you through some of the alternatives, which do you feel you would like to go for?

This question is 46 words long and any patient hearing it would probably reply with 'Um. Would you mind repeating that?'

A better question would be:

> Now we've talked through the drug options, which one do you feel you would go for?

This question is only 16 words long and would be much easier to understand.

Some of the most powerful questions are around 4–5 words long, and in general we suggest keeping questions to 6–12 words. Examples:

> What's your priority here?
>
> What do you want, ideally?
>
> What do you need to know about this?

Avoid double questions: they are confusing. Example:

> When did this symptom start and how much pain are you getting?

These are two separate questions and need to be asked separately. When you ask two questions at once you will typically only get a reply to one of them, thus missing vital information.

## Avoiding 'why?' questions

Avoid using questions which begin with *why*. 'Why' is an open question, but unfortunately it can have overtones of rebuke and usually leads to the non-answer 'I don't know':

> I want to ask you now about your treatment, and I am particularly interested in why you haven't been taking your medication and why you have been having side effects.

This is a poor-quality question as it contains two uses of the word *why*, and is also a double question.

This would be a better question:

> You say you stopped taking the pills. Tell me about how you got on with them.

This version combines a subtle summary showing the patient that they have been heard, and then a brief open question which invites honest disclosure.

In general the most powerful questions begin with the word *what* or *how*. This is because they cannot be answered *yes* or *no* and are more likely to draw out high-quality replies.

Compare these two versions of questions asking a patient how she has got on with her medication:

Did you get on all right with those pills I prescribed?

How did you get on with those pills I prescribed?

The first version  suggests that the right answer is 'yes'. Patients may dissemble or lie rather than tell you the truth. The second version is far more likely to encourage the patient to disclose what has really happened, for instance, experiencing side effects, reluctance to take pills for prophylactic reasons or failing to complete the course because they felt better.

Silence is often a sign that you have asked an excellent question – do not feel the need to follow on immediately with another question or paraphrase to fill the space. Just wait and see what happens.

Examples of other good questions include:

How committed are you to this goal?

If all the obstacles disappeared, what would you do?

If our roles were reversed, what would you be asking right now?

What could you start doing/stop doing which would help your situation?

What else is going on in your life that it might be useful for me to know about?

What do you care about the most?

What would need to happen to … ?

What do you want the outcome to be?

What help do you want/would you most value from me?

## Avoiding jargon

All clinicians are warned during initial training about the importance of avoiding jargon, yet somehow it creeps back in. Jargon and technical language are unhelpful and alienating in a clinical consultation. It doesn't help you or the patient to get the best from the time you have available and only serves to emphasize the clinician-as-expert role. Simplify the messages you give to patients and borrow clues from them in the language they chose when discussing their health. For example, a common side effect of starting antidepressants is that they can disturb the gut. The jargon-filled way to describe this would be:

> 25 per cent of people experience gastrointestinal side effects which include nausea, and anorexia but it passes after 72 hours.

Compare this with the simplicity of:

> About a quarter of people feel slightly sick and off their food when they start this medicine, but this usually passes after a few days.

## Clean language

Clean language is a specific conversational technique which aims to open up the conversation further and to boost rapport. Described first by the therapist David Grove,[8] it draws on the observation that we often use similes and metaphors in our conversational speech, and that these can provide valuable insights to our thinking if explored. For example, a patient may say 'I feel at sea' or 'I feel lost' during a conversation about depression. They do not mean that they are literally at sea and they do not believe that they are literally lost, but these descriptions vividly convey their sense of futility and isolation. By exploring these metaphors further, you can powerfully demonstrate to the patient that you are curious to get more insight into their world. This can also help the patient to understand their own complex and sometimes contradictory feelings more fully. The principle of clean language is simple – you do not assume that you know what a patient means with the language they choose, but instead you use the language as a cue to explore the emotional dimensions of the patient's experience.

Here is an example of using the clean language approach in a clinical consultation. Lizzie is talking to her primary care physician about her job and how it has contributed to her recent depression:

> 'I feel like I am trapped in a prison, and I can't get out. It's horrible.'
>
> The clinician asks 'What kind of prison is this prison?'
>
> 'It's dank, it's dark, it's a dungeon, says Lizzie.

The clinician says, 'Tell me a bit more about that'.

Lizzie says that although she has just been promoted, she is overwhelmed by the demands of the new role and doubts her competence. 'I feel like the job is my jailer', she says.

'And that's like…?' says the clinician.

'It's like I've put myself in this dungeon.'

'And?'

'And actually', says Lizzie, looking up for the first time, 'there's no key, I'm being my own jailer, I could walk away'.

This brief exchange was powerful. Lizzie felt heard at a deep level. She realized that it was within her own control to decide whether she stayed in the job or not and her depression began to lift from that point on.

Some questions we have found useful are:

And what kind of — is that?

And where does that — come from?

And that's like…what?

And what happens next?

And is there anything else about —?

Let's talk more about —.

What does — mean to you?

And if you had/were — what would I see happening?

It is beyond our scope here to describe clean language in detail. Wendy Sullivan and Judy Rees's book, *Clean Language: Revealing Metaphors and Opening Minds*,[9] gives an accessible summary.

## Keeping language positive

Coaching means paying exquisite attention to the impact of language. A carelessly constructed throw-away comment to a patient can have lasting impact:

My daughter has a genetic eye condition. One of her doctors said, 'She will always have some visual impairment.' This had an instantly depressing impact. How different this could have been if the doctor had said 'She will always have a degree of useful vision'.

I presented with a lump in my breast. The doctor immediately said, 'How could you have left it this long?' This comment led to tremendous worry, remorse and guilt on my part and when I thought it over, I realized it was completely unnecessary and unhelpful. My doctor seemed to want to chastise me, but a more helpful comment at this point might have been 'I'm glad you've come to have this looked at now'.

Even with the best of intentions, there can be unfortunate consequences when clinicians are unaware of the nuances of their tone and language, overlook how anxious patients can be and at the same time fail to create rapport, as this patient describes:

I'm no stranger to smear tests having had many over the years following two diagnoses of pre-cancerous cells of the cervix in my twenties. Nevertheless I still felt vulnerable and nervous as I lay in the treatment room while the nurse prepared the instruments. She then began to talk to me in what felt like a severely chiding tone. She told me how women make it unnecessarily hard for themselves by not doing what she tells them. Inevitably I tensed as the examination began. The pain that followed was the worst I have ever experienced while having a smear test. When the nurse next spoke it was to tell me that I was bleeding, that she could not continue with the test, that I would have to come back another time, that I should book a double appointment and ask for the smallest instrument available. Her manner was punitive, implying that it was entirely my fault. My humiliation was complete. I did not book another appointment.

In contrast, a couple of months later, I was having a yearly hospital check up with my gynaecologist. I have been a long-term sufferer of endometriosis and the surgeon had seen me during acute episodes and had operated on me several times. I told her what had happened during the smear test. She just nodded quietly and invited me to hop up on to the couch saying that it was no problem to do the test straight away. Her tone was warm and supportive. She told me exactly what she was going to do, when, and what I could expect. It was so much easier to relax. It was completely pain free. The test was completed with competence and care and my dignity and confidence were restored.

It matters how we present information, even when it is difficult or challenging to give. This doctor describes a patient who was dying of oesophageal cancer and who was becoming increasingly symptomatic, finding it difficult to play the flute, a hobby that had previously brought great pleasure as it enabled her to socialize and take part in a small ensemble:

> I told her that even with the cancer advancing, it was likely she would have many good days during which she would be less symptomatic and would be able to play, albeit for short periods of time. I know, because I heard it direct from her and from her family, that this imparted all-important hope at a time when there was little to be cheerful about. This patient played on and off until 2 weeks before her death.

## Active listening

Most clinicians will have received some training in the scrupulously attentive technique known as *active listening*.

### What gets in the way of real listening?

Sometimes in time-poor consultations these skills can be compromised and we take shortcuts. For instance, when you are experienced you may believe you already know what the diagnosis or treatment should be, even though you have not asked all the questions that would confirm that this is the case. You may be wedded to a particular way of explaining vague symptoms, for instance that they are stress-related. You may enjoy explaining for its own sake ('shall I just draw you a picture of how your knee works?') or miss the clues that a patient gives you through repeated emphasis on particular words and phrases. The computer on your desk may lure you into gazing at it because you are preoccupied with reading the patient's notes and then with entering new ones. When this happens you will miss the data that the patient is offering you just by being there: how they are sitting, their facial expression, tone of voice.

When you are fully and completely engaged in listening to another person, your body language will take care of itself. However, here are some simple techniques to try. They all increase the chances that you and the patient will be fully engaged in the conversation:

- Match the patient's tone, pace and volume of speech to show you are in tune with them.
- Make sure that you use your own body language and gestures to convey your attention, for example by nodding occasionally, smiling and using other facial expressions to convey understanding.
- Note your posture and make sure it is open and inviting but does not intrude on the patient's physical space; so, for example, if the patient is leaning back in their chair, avoid leaning into their space.
- Encourage the patient to continue by making small verbal comments like 'Go on' or 'I'm with you'. Note that you are not necessarily agreeing with the patient, but instead validating that you have heard what they have said.

### Taking patients' questions seriously

The patient's questions provide valuable clues: they are windows into their current concerns.

> I asked about the renal side effects of a medication that I had been prescribed and the reply was 'I don't think you want a lecture on the anatomy of the human kidney do you?' I found this unbelievably patronizing, invalidating my legitimate concerns.

A far better question here might have been:

> That's a good question and it could need a long answer, but how much information would you like to have?

There is more on giving information in Chapter 5.

## Summarizing and reflecting back

One of the most powerful ways to demonstrate connection is to give patients evidence that what they are saying is being heard and synthesized. Summarizing involves careful listening and then using the patient's own language, listening for key words and ideas without embellishing or interpreting what you have heard by adding your own spin. It sounds easy, but in our experience it is a more subtle and complex skill than it may appear at first sight. Inexperienced clinician-coaches often end up forgetting important chunks of what they have heard, making inaccurate assumptions or else parroting back verbatim what their patient has said. Summarizing and reflecting back can also be useful when a patient presents a lot of complex information in a short space of time, and you need to pause to take stock of what they are saying, especially if you are getting confused yourself.

For example:

> You've told me about lots of problems with the new medication, but it sounds like there are two main issues. The first is that you feel sleepy in the mornings and the second is that you've developed a rash.

Some of these prompts may be helpful as ways of interrupting a patient to take stock:

> So let me just stop you for a minute, and see if I have understood the main issues. It seems like you are saying three main things....

> I am getting a bit lost here, can I just try and summarize?

> Have I understood you correctly? It seems like you are mainly saying ...

> So you feel... ?

Always end a summary with 'Have I got that right?' or 'Have I understood you correctly?'. This is an open invitation to the patient to add to what they have already said, or to correct you if you have got something wrong. If you have misunderstood, even where the patient feels overawed by hierarchy and status, most patients will come back with 'Well actually, it's not quite like that, it's more...'. This is because with an active listening style you have shown a willingness to be corrected and a genuine desire to understand.

In terms of other verbal boosters of rapport, choose the patient's own words when describing their difficulty, for instance, 'How long have you been feeling sick?' rather than 'How long have you had the nausea?'.

## Feedback in the here and now

This skill involves close observation of what is happening in the consultation and feeding it back to the patient, for instance about observing more energy, less energy, little pauses and hesitations or repeated use of certain words or phrases.

In this example the patient was a young woman with long-standing health issues, challenging social circumstances, was six months pregnant and being abused by her partner. The doctor describes feeling initially as overwhelmed as the patient:

> I was at a loss about how to proceed, but instead of getting sucked down into despair along with the patient, I asked 'What's going right here?' At this point in the consultation, the body language of the patient changed completely – she was clearly enormously proud of her developing baby and awaited her arrival with hope and gladness. I fed back to her the change in the way she was sitting, speaking, and holding herself and I know it was a big thing for the patient to have heard that. It led onto a much more productive and focused conversation about how she would manage things once her daughter arrived.

This simple acknowledgement that you are in tune with the patient, and that you can feed back what you see in the room at the time to benefit both of you is enormously powerful. Some of these examples may be helpful:

> I've noticed that when you talked about XX, your body language changed and you [describe what you see]. What's going on for you?

> While we have been talking I've noticed that you've mentioned XX several times, and you seem to be very focused on it. I'm wondering if it's important to explore XX a bit more?

> It feels like when we were talking about XX, the energy has gone from your voice and your body. I am wondering what's behind that.

## Exploring blocks and barriers

The patient is resolute that he will stop smoking after his beloved father died of lung cancer, he is adamant that he has smoked his last cigarette, yet he returns to you smoking 40 cigarettes a day two months later. Or there might be the obese patient with early osteoarthritis who signed up for a half marathon with every intention of training three times a week, but instead has given up her place in the race. Because we are dealing with human beings and not automated machines, patients backslide. Perhaps more so than at any other time in the coaching conversation, it will be important to suspend your own judgement and disappointment, and instead be genuinely curious about the origins of their difficulties. The patient may feel shame when they have been unable to follow through on what they have agreed. Your job is to get underneath the shame, and truly understand what is going on. You might ask:

> We agreed last time we met that you would [describe what was agreed] and I notice that you haven't manage to do this yet. What's stopping you?

or

> What's the block?

Sometimes a patient will reveal a self-limiting belief at this point – a belief about themselves as a person, or about their abilities (or alleged lack of them) which holds them back and keeps them stuck. So for instance, the smoker who relapsed, might reply to the question 'What's the block?' with 'I'm useless at sticking with things. I don't have any willpower'; the obese patient with osteoarthritis might reply 'My mother always told me I was a quitter'. Both admissions could lead into fruitful conversations that may ultimately unstick beliefs which hold back progress. (There is more about this in Chapter 4.)

## Summary

Bringing coaching to your clinical practice involves revisiting and honing many of the skills that you have learnt already during training, but which sometimes get obscured and diminished by the realities of twenty-first-century clinical practice. Paying special attention to the beginning of the consultation, thinking about names, choosing language carefully, and drawing on some coaching-specific techniques will allow you to transform routine clinical consultations into time for reflection and progress for you and your patient.

# References

1. Granger, K. *#hellomynameis*. http://hellomynameis.org.uk (accessed 3 November 2014).
2. Granger, K. I want my legacy to be that the NHS treats all patients with compassion. *The Guardian*, 2 February 2015. http://www.theguardian.com/healthcare-network/2014/may/21/friendly-introduction-transform-patient-experience. (accessed 12 June 2015).
3. Mateen, F.J. and Dorji, C. Health-care worker burnout and the mental health imperative. *Lancet* 2009; 374(9690): 595–597.
4. Gawande, A. *Being Mortal: Medicine and What Matters in the End*. New York: Metropolitan Books; 2014.
5. Griffin, J. and Tyrrell, I. *Human Givens*. Brighton: HG Publishing; 2004.
6. Karpman, S.B. Fairy tales and script drama analysis. *Transactional Analysis Bulletin* 1968; 7(26): 39–43.
7. Karpman, S.B. and Stephen, B. *A Game Free Life: The Definitive Book on the Drama Triangle and Compassion Triangle by the Originator and Author*. San Francisco: Drama Triangle Publications; 2014.
8. Grove, D. *Philosophy and Principles of Clean Language*; 1998. http://www.cleanlanguage.co.uk/articles/articles/38/1/Philosophy-and-Principles-of-Clean-Language/Page1.html. (accessed 3 November 2014).
9. Sullivan, W. and Rees, J. *Clean Language: Revealing Metaphors and Opening Minds*. Bancyfelin, Carmarthen: Crown House; 2008.

# 4 CHANGING LIFE-LIMITING BEHAVIOUR

A vast amount of clinician time is absorbed by consultations with people whose health problems have been created at least in part by lifestyle choices. In this chapter we look at how to use a coaching approach to trigger better self-care for these patients. The aim is for patients to leave the consultation equipped with belief in their ability to change and with confidence in their own judgement.

Consider the following scenario:

> The scene is a doctor with a very overweight patient. The patient is complaining about painful knees and about chronic chafing between her thighs and under her breasts.
>
> 'My knees hurt all the time and I've got this awful chafing here and here … [points]. It's so uncomfortable and embarrassing and nothing I use on it seems to help –'
>
> The doctor interrupts swiftly. 'What about your weight?'
>
> 'What about it?'
>
> The doctor says politely and evenly that being so very many pounds over the ideal will inevitably cause exactly the problems the patient has.
>
> 'People are just big in my family. My Mum's big and my Nan was big. It's in my genes. There's nothing I can do.'
>
> The doctor is now fidgeting in his chair. His smile is beginning to fade.
>
> 'But there is something you can do', he says. 'I can offer you some fantastic diet sheets. Anyone can lose weight. It's not about genes. It's about what you put in your mouth.'

'Diets don't work for me. I've tried everything, I did Weight Watchers off and on for years and then I did Lighter Life and lost 6 stone but all that happens is that I pile it back on again – and more.'

And so the consultation goes miserably on. The doctor makes suggestions, the patient counters with, 'yes, but...'. It ends with the doctor's colour rising, he is visibly only just containing his frustration and at one point even wagging his finger at the patient, accompanying this with dire warnings about how her health will worsen dramatically unless she changes her eating habits and takes more exercise.

The patient leaves without the diet sheet.

This was a role-played exchange at a training course with a skilled actor role-playing the patient and the doctor playing himself, recreating the kind of consultation, based on an actual patient, that he had chosen because he had found it especially taxing. As this doctor said in the review and replay of the video, dumbstruck by the accurate way the actor had reproduced the 'patient', 'This is exactly how it is! I can't bear it! Why do these patients do this? Why won't they let me help them?'

In the discussion following this episode, the group, actor and doctor agreed that, brilliant though the actor had been, it was nothing much to do with her and everything to do with the doctor who had faithfully reproduced his own typical behaviour. He had intruded with his own agenda instead of working to the one presented by the patient, he had interrupted, he had stopped listening, he had done 80 per cent of the talking; he had reproached and lectured. Perversely, he had made absolutely certain that the 'patient' would reject his well-meant advice.

## Looking yourself in the eye

As clinicians we are drawn to our professions because we want to feel that we have made a difference. We want to make our knowledge available, we want our patients' lives to improve. And where better to be helpful than in working with patients on preventable illnesses caused by potentially life-limiting habits such as disordered eating, smoking, drinking too much alcohol, neglecting oral hygiene, reckless sexual behaviour, taking too little exercise, using sunbeds, taking illegal drugs or getting the balance between work and play hopelessly askew? If you could read the minds of some typically frustrated practitioners during these exchanges, this is what they would say:

> How can I persuade this guy that he's already had several problematical moles and that however bad his psoriasis, using sun beds every week is hugely raising his risks of skin cancer and he should stop?

> She is 20 kilos overweight and takes no exercise. No wonder she's hypertensive.

> I must get this man to see that if he doesn't stop binge-drinking his liver will pack up.

> Her irresponsible sexual behaviour puts her in the high risk category for cervical cancer and STDs. She just must have screening. Why is she refusing?

This way of thinking is characterized by the black-and-white language of command and control: *must, irresponsible, persuade, stop*. It is underpinned by a wish to reform the patient. It leads to strong temptation to tell and direct, and sometimes to threaten ('Do you want to die young?'), turning the clinician role into one which seems to be about policing 'bad' behaviour with attendant threats of punishments (pain, disability, death).

Other clinicians are genuinely moved by seeing the severe toll that poor lifestyle choices, combined with poverty and bad luck, is taking on their patients:

> I felt such compassion for him: only last year he had been a man in a reasonably well-paid job, now he looked grubby and pathetic, he was reliant on handouts from a food bank and other charities, living in a hostel and had taken up smoking again. Stopping smoking seemed to me like the easiest way for him to regain self-respect and I was willing to go all out to help him.

> It was obvious to me that she might lose her kids unless she stopped drinking. As a mother myself, I felt so sorry for her, I kept imaging how that would feel if it were me. I was desperate to persuade her to join our Sensible Drinkers group.

Compassion is a noble emotion, but if it moves from kindness and empathy to pity, it is an essentially unhelpful frame of mind, leading to a wish to rescue the patient, for instance by doing things for them that they could do for themselves, thus undermining them and unwittingly conveying disrespect. The give-away here is the intensity of the language: *pathetic, sorry for, go all out to help, desperate to persuade.*

Sometimes these patients arouse uncomfortable feelings: they seem dislikeable, they are wasting our time with their self-generated problems, many of which seem to create the opportunity for the clinician to feel morally superior. Prejudice against smoking or obesity is widespread and there has been speculation that some clinicians may miss an obvious diagnosis, for instance of asthma in a very overweight patient complaining of breathlessness, because of an assumption that the cause must be obesity. The general discourse in parts of the tabloid press about 'scroungers' and immigrants 'swamping' our services might also easily contaminate our thinking:

> This woman, is, I know, dirt poor and doesn't speak good English. She lives in a very overcrowded house and doesn't really have access to a cooker. Yet I still found myself wondering why she is eating such rubbish food and why she whines to me in every consultation about things I can do nothing about.

> He is so fat that he can only just walk and can barely squash himself into the patient's chair. Sweat pours down his face and back. Honestly I find it difficult to look at him.

What can be happening here is what some schools of therapy describe as *projection*. When we see something about ourselves that we fear or know might be true of us, we project it on to others. Like everyone else, clinicians can have problems with impulse control, or with alcohol, sexual behaviour, drug addiction and weight. How much easier it is to dislike the patient and to want to reform them rather than to dislike or reform ourselves. It can be difficult to own up to these feelings privately, let alone acknowledge them to others. Clinicians are trained in detachment, and this includes detachment from our own feelings. It can be challenging to come to terms with feelings that frighten us by their intensity. As the American writer and psychiatrist, James Groves,[1] wrote in a famous article published many decades ago but from which he still gets regular correspondence:

What is it about the patient 'everybody hates' that compromises [the physician's] workaday skills? It is probably the additional burden of having to deny or disown the intense, hateful feelings kindled by the dependent, entitled, manipulative or self-destructive patient ... When the patient creates in the doctor feelings that are disowned or denied, errors in diagnosis and treatment are more likely to occur. Disavowal of hateful feelings requires less effort than bearing them.

It is easy to forget when patients arouse these feelings that the causes of lifestyle problems are socially complex; they are broader than just 'individual responsibility'. For instance, where obesity is concerned there is the abundance of advertising for fatty, sugary, salty foods, there is the ubiquity of cheap fast food, the trebling of typical portion size in the last six decades, and the disproportionate rise in food prices relative to incomes in poorer households.

Added to this there can be government pressure with those positively intentioned public health campaigns such as *Making Every Contact Count*,[2] plus in some cases financial incentives to tick boxes to signify that patients have been asked certain questions. This could mean that in many cases clinicians raise lifestyle issues that come from their and not the patient's agenda and assume that the 'solution' is simple – the patient should simply stop doing the 'wrong' behaviour and start being virtuous.

## The short-term thinking of the human species

There is nothing too surprising or different about patients with lifestyle issues, and there are biological as well as psychological issues at play here. As neuroscience – and the even newer science of behavioural economics – makes clear, as a species we seem to be programmed for immediate gratification because our brains, still essentially as they were in the Stone Age, prefer choices that give us a rapid return. Many of our decisions are based on irrational feelings and beliefs (see also Chapter 2), not on what might be dictated by logic and facts.[3]

We tend to exclude uncomfortable data. So we overestimate our likely lifespan, we fudge the question of how much alcohol we drink, we do not face our lack of exercise, promising ourselves that we will take up running, or walking, or swimming 'next week'. One UK study[4] involving 650 people investigated how far people with a BMI of over 30 saw themselves as 'obese' or, in less stigmatizing words, 'very overweight'. Only 11 per cent of the women and 7 per cent of the men considered that this described them. The implication is that these people will not identify with health messages on the subject of weight. Nor does it help to try inducing shame. There is a common perception, for instance, that 'fat shaming' might encourage weight loss, but the research suggests that, if anything, it makes the problem worse: one study[5] showed that obese people who experienced discrimination and harassment in public actually gained weight over a four-year period.

The natural human tendency is towards inertia – continuing doing what we have always done and being reluctant to seek new information. Our brains prefer the status quo[6] because it takes up more energy to generate new habits than to persist with old ones, even when we know that doing so will create problems. As a species we also seem prone to 'hyperbolic discounting',[7] meaning that we will tend to choose a small immediate reward over a larger one that will only happen at some point in the future, and the further into the future it is, the more likely it is that we will ignore its implications for the present. We prefer speedily made decisions which feel effortless, but may be wrong, to slower ones which literally use more brain power but will give a more accurate result.

Where information is known to be complex, or there seem to be too many options with apparently contradictory evidence involved, we can fear making the wrong choices and become paralysed by indecision. The Nobel prize-winner Daniel Kahneman has written a bestselling book, *Thinking, Fast and Slow*,[8] which offers a summary of the evidence in this area. All of this applies as much to eating, smoking, drinking as to the other decisions looked at by behavioural economists where they have shown through innumerable experiments that we are easily persuaded by illogical factors even when we believe we are quirky individualists immune to such blandishments.[9]

## The impact on patients

In earlier chapters we described the evidence which clearly shows that telling, directing and trying to impose information on people are pointless as ways of influencing them. The motto here is: *clinicians insist, patients resist*. Very few people with conditions caused by or linked to lifestyle choices are unaware of what they should be doing. They feel shame, they fear criticism and can feel reproached even when nothing is said overtly:

'Oh it's you again,' the receptionist said. She was scowling at me. I watched her look me up and down and saw 'fat cow' in her face. I took from that she had heard from her colleagues that if only I'd stop eating chocolate I wouldn't be wasting everyone's time.

A middle-aged straight man talking to a young gay man about sex: his face was perfectly neutral but I felt disapproval radiating from him and I just knew I'd be getting the talking-to about STDs and AIDS – did he really think I didn't already know all of that?

I routinely put off seeing the dental hygienist. I can't bear his look of weary reproach when I have once again 'failed' to keep to his regime.

I went to my doctor with a painful infection around a fingernail. Literally the first words out of his mouth were, 'Are you still smoking?' I wanted help with the nail, not to get yet another round of questioning on when I was going to give up smoking and how bad it was for people with Raynaud's.

When patients feel like this they are much less likely to return, and the chances are that they will do so only when their problems have intensified, have become more complex and therefore trickier, more time-consuming and more costly to treat.

## Fear and health

How do you motivate people to change their behaviour? How much does it help if you frighten them? These questions have preoccupied advertisers and politicians as well as public health campaigners, since there is big money at stake in knowing the answers. More than 50 years of research shows the pattern and it is a subtle and complex one.[10] It seems that if the fear threat is only moderate, vaguely expressed or from a source that the recipient does not find credible then fear is not motivating. If the threat can create high levels of fear but there is no companion message about how it can be immediately and comprehensively reduced, then the typical response is avoidance: flinching and then ignoring. So parents telling teenagers that smoking may take ten years off their lives is unlikely to change behaviour because the threat is too vague and too far into the future to have meaning and to a teenager a parent is probably not a credible source.

This is the formula:

> credible source + well-evidenced immediate severe threat to health + easily adopted ways of resolving the threat + social support = success.

Here is how one doctor skilfully used this formula, as recounted by her patient:

> We were on very good terms and I felt she liked me. I know she's on my side but it was a shock to have the post-hospital-tests session. She told me that the chronic pain in my legs was atherosclerosis, that my breathlessness had to be taken seriously, that the cause was undoubtedly my heavy smoking for 50 years and that the chances of a heart attack or stroke within the next year were very high. Then that I was a good candidate for surgery on the worse one of the legs, that warfarin could reduce the stroke risk, that I would need to control and reduce alcohol, that I needed to give up smoking straight away. Then that she would prescribe nicotine patches plus different BP medication, that I needed to immediately up the amount of walking I was doing even though it was so painful and that if I did all this I would improve my chances of living another ten years by a huge amount. She ended the conversation by reminding me that I was a successful lawyer and that she had observed what she called my 'steeliness' in action and that she was absolutely sure I could make all these changes. I went home, told my wife, and we both became instant non-smokers. I had a huge amount of support from that doc over the following few months and I'm eternally grateful that she was so straightforward with me. That was five years ago and without her intervention I think I would be dead by now.

## Ambivalence about change

Ambivalence is at the heart of human behaviour when it comes to making desirable lifestyle changes. Campaigners for more sensible behaviour often appear to forget that we drink, smoke or take recreational drugs because these are associated with pleasant experiences, or that risky behaviour can create an enjoyable thrill. The hormone and neurotransmitter dopamine seems to be involved here, creating a rush of pleasurable feeling.[11] The memory of that feeling encourages us to seek the same experience again and again, even if ultimately the experience itself, as with many actual addictions, is no longer pleasurable.

Motivational interviewing (MI) practitioners (see also page 32) call it 'change talk'. It means listening hard for signs that a patient may be considering that a change in behaviour is necessary and possible. The trouble is that human change can be complicated. The bigger the change and the more we have invested in our current behaviour, the slower and more gradual the change is likely to be, with many steps between first thoughts about it and actually doing it.

## The Prochaska and DiClemente model of change

James Prochaska and his colleague Carlo DiClemente[12] developed a helpful model which arose originally out of work with people who had problems with alcohol. It acknowledges the reality that health-related change can take time. The model describes six stages from pre-contemplation, where the patient is unaware and totally unready for change, to termination, where the problematical behaviour is no longer an issue (Table 4.1).

There will be 'change talk' associated with each stage. So even with the pre-contemplation stage you may hear phrases like 'One day I might…'. When the patient is at the contemplation stage you might hear wistful comment such as 'I really wish I could…', 'My friend X has recently lost a lot of weight…' or 'I know I'd feel better if I gave up smoking…'. At preparation it will begin to sound more committed with statements such as 'I suppose I could…', 'If I tried, I might…', 'I did once do something like this before and it seemed to work…'.

The action phase is characterized by more dynamic statements where tentative statements involving words like *might* or *could* are replaced by 'I will' and 'My plan is that I will', though look out here for words that suggest the possibility of failure, such as 'I'll try'. This model is a reminder to be alert to the language that patients use. For instance, there is everything to be said for understanding that the questions and comments from you that will work for someone now fiercely committed

**Table 4.1** The Prochaska and DiClemente stages of change model

| | Stage | Typical patient comments | Where practitioners can help |
|---|---|---|---|
| 1 | **Pre-contemplation:** time period, years | Nothing to do with me, it's not a problem, I ignore it, why won't people shut up about it? | Acknowledge the patient's right to this choice. Challenge, but skilfully. Raise awareness that there could be benefits to changing |
| 2 | **Contemplation:** time period, 6 months | I'm thinking about it. I'll do something, but not yet | Validate the patient's thinking, offer encouragement – I'm here when you're ready |
| 3 | **Preparation:** time period, 1 month | It's becoming an issue, I'll explore my options | Encourage; offer support, spell out the practical help available; discuss small steps that could become the start of the change |
| 4 | **Action:** time period, weeks/days | I'm committed, I'll do it | Validate the patient's choice without seeming over-eager; ask the patient to spell out the benefits of staying on course; discuss substitute activities that will distract from old habits; discuss how to replace old habits with new ones. Ask about supporters, encourage declarations to friends and family. |
| 5 | **Maintenance:** time period, 6 months | It got to seem so easy, but unfortunately I've had a few relapses | Acknowledge that relapses are all part of making the change; discuss how to avoid situations and people associated with temptation. Re-discuss the benefits |
| 6 | **Termination** | It's not a problem any more – I don't even think about it | Acknowledge the effort and skill involved without seeming to patronize |

to stopping smoking (action) stand no chance whatsoever of working with someone who is at pre-contemplation. And you might be missing the vital signals that you could work fruitfully with patients who are ready to change (preparation) if you assume, wrongly, that they are stuck at pre-contemplation.

This model is just a framework, and as with any such framework, it is salutary to remember the Zen saying, 'The finger pointing at the Moon is not the Moon'. The model has been criticized by some for what they say is lack of clear proof that it is superior to other approaches.[13] Many patients will not fit neatly into each stage. However, we like this model for the emphasis it puts on acknowledging that change has distinct phases, each with its own opportunities for intervention and clinician support, that change involves balancing gains with losses, that for positive changes to happen and become permanent, the pros need to outweigh the cons at every stage and that backsliding is normal. It encourages us as clinicians to enquire with curiosity and respect into the patient's thinking, offering hope, information, the belief that healthier behaviour could be a part of who they are and conveying our confidence in their ability to change for the better.

## Secrets of success

If telling and directing do not work, then what does? Research into MI has shown that when as a clinician you follow a step-by-step process similar to the one we describe below you will increase your chances of working successfully with these patients. People are more likely, for instance, to stay in treatment, to take part in needle-exchange schemes, improve their diets, follow oral hygiene protocols, give up smoking, reduce use of illegal drugs and reduce excess weight. They will also tend to have fewer subsequent hospital admissions. You can find a regularly updated summary of the research at www.motivationalinterviewing. org.

### Being clear with the patient about your own point of view

You do not have to disguise your own viewpoint, and there will be a place at some point in the initial consultation to say straightforwardly that you believe it would be a good idea for the patient to change the risky or undesirable behaviour. This is honest and is also a guard against a patient who disingenuously claims later that 'the doctor/nurse/dentist/ physio never told me it was wrong'. A single statement, informally, neutrally and calmly phrased, is usually enough. These work best when they are put in a positive form in terms of the benefits patients will gain rather than as threats. Examples we have collected include statements such as:

> I'm a dentist so of course I'm going to tell you that better oral hygiene will increase the chances of keeping your own teeth for life – and I can show you how simple it is to do.

> You will see immediate changes in things like reduced breathlessness and food tasting better within a few days of stopping smoking.

> I'm sure, and this is based on my own experience and training, that carrying so much extra weight is definitely putting you at increased risk of developing heart disease.

> We can't do anything about our genes, but it's pretty certain that halving your alcohol intake will increase your chances of avoiding some of the nastier cancers.

### Emphasizing that you know the decision always lies with the patient

You may take this for granted, but you cannot assume that the patient knows that this is your position. Paradoxically, by emphasizing that you know it is their decision, you reduce resistance to change. Useful statements here might include:

> I know it can feel as if you're under a lot of pressure to make this change, but only you can make that decision.

> No one can live your life for you and in the end it's totally down to you what you do.

> It's entirely your choice, but I want you to know that I'm here to support you when you feel ready.

> A lot of people feel like you at the beginning of a change like this and you have to weigh it all up for yourself because you know yourself better than anyone else.

> I can make suggestions but in the end it's what will work for you that matters.

## Identifying the pay-off

When you look below the surface of unwise behaviour you will usually find that the causes go beyond the apparent simplicities of 'greed' or 'lack of willpower', as these thoughtful clinicians describe:

> My patient was obsessed with 'extreme sports' despite admitting to not having the skills or physique to take part in them safely. He had a history of serious injuries, including damaged his spleen in a paragliding accident. In clinic after yet another fracture, he told me he was proposing getting involved in BASE jumping. On the face of it this was asking for death. The explanation? During the week he was a reluctant but loving stay-at-home dad with no outlet for his need for thrills and risk.

> Her binge eating was all to do with the excessive demands she put on herself by putting everyone's needs before her own. After everyone else had gone to bed she'd wolf down three or four packets of biscuits, or several tins of sweetcorn and tuna with a whole loaf of bread despite telling me that she was never actually hungry at that point. I asked her, 'what are you hungry for then?' and her reply was stark: 'Love and attention'.

> Dan saw smoking as his only treat in a demanding life doing boring low-paid work. 'It's time for me, it's time for me' was his mantra.

> This patient readily owned up to drinking a bottle of wine every evening. She told me straight that it was about what she called 'anaesthetizing' herself because life was unbearable after the death of her 20-year-old daughter and the subsequent break up of her marriage.

The secret here is to ask yourself what problem the undesirable behaviour is appearing to solve for the patient, so, as in the examples above, the answers may be that overeating provides fleeting comfort or that alcohol temporarily blots out loneliness. So the clinician motto here might be: first identify the pay-off. Only then can you proceed to solutions. Ask questions such as:

> What's the pay-off here? What do you get out of it?

> What is it you enjoy about [smoking, drinking, drugs, … ]?

When you do this you are taking several steps simultaneously that can be powerful for patients. First you are asking them to make their thinking visible and you will not be able to work with them effectively unless this has happened. You are giving them the opportunity to tell you about underlying causes that go beyond the apparent simplicities of gluttony, self-indulgence or ignorance to explain their behaviour. You are showing that you accept patients because you are not going to be shocked by what they tell you.

Changing behaviour may also be associated in the patient's mind with real or anticipated discomfort: aching muscles after unaccustomed exercise, facing chronic boredom, experiencing the hunger pangs associated with dieting or psychological cravings for alcohol or tobacco.

## Hunting the discount

Each patient is at a different stage on the journey to a healthier life. Many clinicians have found that there is considerable merit in using an approach adopted from transactional analysis, a set of theories about personality and also a form of psychotherapy (see also page 53). TA suggests the idea that disrupting dysfunctional habits is problematical and that what we do is to deny reality and give ourselves excuses for resisting change. TA calls these excuses *discounts*. Identifying the discount will save many fruitless conversations with patients. They form a kind of ladder of blockage, and for each one there is a different way of responding.

### This isn't a problem

This discount is like the pre-contemplation stage of the Prochaska and DiClemente model. It is about refusing to believe that there is a problem. Some examples: the smoker believes that the evidence against tobacco has been manufactured by do-gooders; the obese person has read somewhere that fat people actually live just as long as thin ones; the heavy drinker tells you that 'research shows' that people in France drink more than they do in other European countries but that their rates of liver disease are lower; the non-exerciser tells you that runners get arthritis.

Good questions to ask here might be:

What do you know for certain about the facts?

How reliable do you believe the evidence is?

Might you be up for some additional information here, for instance (depending on the patient and their familiarity with the internet) some useful websites?

## It may be generally true but it won't affect me

There is a good deal of evidence[14] to suggest that as human beings we often have an overoptimistic view of how far our behaviour puts us at risk. For instance, many obese people underestimate how overweight they are and fail to see that their own weight puts them in the danger category; smokers will put a positive spin on their chances of developing lung cancer. Others may be too young to be able to envisage their lives more than a few years ahead and offer you the 'life's too short' version of this discount, or they may say that they agree they should give up smoking but now is not the time. One explanation here is that because people are currently asymptomatic they may conclude that they are unlikely to develop the problem in the future. Others may have a sense of personal invulnerability – 'it can happen to others but not to me'.

> I saw a patient who was a heavy smoker, on 30 cigarettes a day, and he told me he was well aware of the potential problems people can suffer because of smoking, but that he was confident he would not be affected. When I asked him what made him think that, he replied that his father was also a heavy smoker who was told the same thing, yet he continued to smoke till he passed away at the age of 95. As his father lived a very long life despite the smoking, my patient had concluded that he must have good genes and would therefore be protected!

This discount is a little like the pre-contemplation stage of the Prochaska and DiClemente model

Useful questions or comments here might be:

> It's good to have an optimistic outlook, but that doesn't necessarily prevent us contracting the conditions associated with [whatever the unhealthy habit might be].

What's the rest of the family history here?

Who do you know who didn't beat the odds?

One way of looking at it is that, yes, you stand a 90 per cent chance of not developing lung cancer in the next ten years, but that there is a 10 per cent chance that you will. Does that put a different spin on it for you?

What do you know about the things you can do that help protect against developing these problems?

### None of the things that work for other people will work for me

This discount has some resemblance to the Prochaska and DiClemente contemplation and preparation stages. It may be the one that you encounter most often. The patient recognizes their risk and their doubts are all to do with having tried and failed. You will hear generalizations such as 'People like me just don't have the willpower', 'I tried hypnosis but I was awake the whole time', 'People who go on diets just put more back on, don't they?' and 'My friend told me that tobacco is more addictive than heroin, so what chance do I have? No wonder I've never managed to stop for more than a few days'.

Powerful questions come into their own here, for instance:

When you've tried before, what worked, even if it was just for a short time?

When you've seen friends do this, what has worked for them?

Who are your supporters here?

What might you try that's different this time, just as a first step?

It is particularly important to avoid asking the question why (see also page 60), as in 'But *why* can't you just give it a try?', as this will invariably seem like a command in disguise or an accusation. The most likely response is a shrug or 'I don't know'.

### It's no good, I can't change

With this discount, what has happened is that the patient has convinced themselves that even though they accept the risks and know the likely solutions, they deeply doubt their own ability to change. Often this discount is about fear that they could not live with the consequences of change. So, for instance, the smoker fears being unable to have a tricky phone call without a cigarette to hand, the solitary drinker fears the tedium of a lonely evening at home without alcohol, the inveterate club-ber is afraid of looking different or of being bored without illegal drugs to provide faux excitement.

Many of the same questions that work with other types of discount will also work here, but additionally valuable questions are:

If you imagine you've made the change, how would it feel?

What would be the overall benefits of the changes you'd like to make?

If you imagine for a moment that you could cope, what would be going on for you?

## Agree a goal for each consultation

Typically a clinical consultation starts with a bland question such as 'What can I do for you today?' or even nothing – waiting for the patient to say what they want. Some clinicians believe they are already agree-ing a goal when they ask questions like 'Did you stick to that diet plan we agreed last time?'.

This is not a genuine goal-setting question because it comes from the clinician's agenda and conveys the idea that you are policing the patient. It has a flavour of interrogation and the reply is likely to involve equiv-ocation or defensiveness, such as 'Um. Well it's a bit tricky because the canteen at work only does fry-ups and …', followed by more reasons why it has been hard.

This kind of reply may tempt you into admonishing the patient or repeating your advice that losing weight is 'essential'.

A much more productive conversation would go like this:

| | |
|---|---|
| *Clinician:* | We agreed a diet plan last time. I'm interested to know how you've been getting on. |
| *Patient:* | So-so. Some of it's worked and some of it hasn't. It's difficult at lunch time because the canteen just offers fry-ups and I don't have time to get out and search for something healthier. |

> Clinician: Yes, I can see that might be an issue. but I'm glad to hear that some of it worked and I'd like to hear more about that in a moment. But what should we focus on today?
>
> Patient: Maybe get your advice on what to put in a packed lunch would be useful and give me a bit of a boot up the backside to organize it because I know I could!

Here the clinician starts by showing interest in how the patient has got on with the actions agreed at the last consultation and gets a typical admission that while it has been possible to stick to the diet sometimes, at others, the temptation of the lunchtime fry-ups has been irresistible. The clinician shows interest in hearing about what has worked. The goal-setting question is 'What should we focus on today?' – asking for the patient's agenda. The patient responds by naming a topic that can be easily dealt with inside a brief consultation.

Behaviour change is best thought of as a journey where it is likely that you will see the same patient several times. For each one, agreeing a goal for the consultation will greatly increase the chances of the patient making the change. Goal-setting is one of the most studied areas of human behaviour.[15] It is clear that setting a goal that you negotiate is more powerful than one set by someone else, that a small, specific, achievable goal that also has some degree of challenge in it is more motivating than a massive one, and that putting it in the positive is more motivating than putting it in the negative. So, for instance, 'being slim' (a going-towards goal) is a better goal than 'losing weight' (a getting-away-from-something goal). A good all-purpose question which is designed to elicit a positive response is:

What would you like to be able to do that you can't do now?

This dietician describes the radical impact that asking this question had on Wesley, a young and extremely overweight patient:

> Until I had learnt the value of a genuine goal-setting question I'd go round and round getting nowhere with patients like Wesley.

He'd just look down and mumble something about hating being so fat, hating people mocking him on buses, hating being dependent on his mum. But when I said, 'So tell me Wesley, what's one thing, even if it's very small, that you'd like to be able to do that you can't do now? Long pause. Then he looked up shyly and said, 'I'd like to be able to put my own socks on'. That was the beginning of unlocking everything in my work with him.

Getting clarity on what the patient wants is the key:

With my smoking cessation patients, after the initial greeting, I now say something like, 'So let's catch up on where you are? How is it going?' Then, depending on their reply, I'll say, 'So what would it be most useful for us to concentrate on today?' Usually it turns out to be something quite specific like 'I'm wondering if you can prescribe that drug that stops the craving', or 'I'm using vaping as a substitute but I read something on the internet about how it's not really going to get me to stop longer term and I'm worried about that – I wanted your advice'.

Do not be afraid to clarify a statement that is too big or too imprecise to be a workable goal:

I find a lot of patients are a bit vague at first. Today I saw someone who has had a scare about her heart and came back from an emergency admission with the message that her weight was 'a problem'. We spent a few minutes discussing the notes from the hospital, which she had also received. Her first response to my question about how I could help was 'I really need to lose six stone'. I knew that was OK as an overall goal, but just so overwhelming in the immediate future. So I said, 'Yes, that's fantastic that you're thinking so hard about it and longer term I agree that would be desirable and it will be a long process, so how would you like to use the time today?' The answer was that she wanted to get my views on whether or not she would be a candidate for bariatric surgery and if so what would be involved. That was relatively easy – she went away happy with what proved to be the very first step on a very long road.

Never underestimate the impact that genuine goal-setting can have as a reliable sign that you are committed to a working partnership. It can transform the patient's willingness to commit to action:

I knew that dental implants could be tricky for me because I had so much bone loss in my mouth. In the initial consultation, the implantologist sat me down in an ordinary chair close to and facing his exactly matching ordinary chair with no desk between us and, after shaking hands and welcoming me, said, 'Now, what do you need to get out of this consultation?' I was immediately reassured because I had expected to be plonked straightaway into the dental chair then to get a hard sell and lots of information. My instant reply was, 'I need you to help me decide whether implants are possible for me, what the risks are, how much pain there would be and what it would cost'. But actually because of that question and the scrupulously honest and careful way he answered it, I had already decided to trust him and to go with it, if, after examination and tests, he thought it was possible. It was, and I did, with excellent results.

## Sticking to the positive

It is easy to underestimate the effect of the actual words we use. Language can have an immediate impact on mood, so the language the patient uses him- or herself is as important as the language of the clinician (see also pages 62 and 114). When patients are struggling with behaviour change, the clinician-coach encourages positive rather than negative language. Clinicians can learn here from skilled salespeople who will do everything they can to avoid letting a potential buyer make 'objections' ('It's too expensive', 'I don't like the colour', 'I'm not quite ready to buy yet', 'I want a different size'). This is because hearing yourself say these negatives makes it a lot less likely that you will buy. The expert clinician-coach also avoids letting the patient talk about their doubts. So rather than encourage the patient to express the reasons for staying the same, it is better to ask questions such as:

What would you get out of giving up [smoking/drug misuse/overeating...]?

Follow up by asking such questions as:

Of those things, which would be most important to you?

What matters to you most about [losing weight, becoming a non-smoker, getting regular dental checks, ...]?

How would you know you were ready?

What would it do for you if you achieved those changes?

What would improve for you if you [took a little more exercise, changed your diet, took the medication every day, ...]?

## Expressing personal concern

Expressing concern can be an underused approach with patients who need to change their behaviour in order to improve their health. By *concern* we do not mean *pity*, or even its non-patronizing cousin *compassion*. There are many thin lines to navigate here. If you seem overinvolved, the patient may back away in alarm. If you appear to be sorrowfully suggesting that you do not wish to be at the patient's funeral, you will annoy. If you appear inauthentic then the patient will dismiss what you say. But genuinely expressed human concern can be powerful:

> I knew I was overweight but I was not facing it. My doctor never uttered a word of reproach to me but what triggered a compelling wish to start a ruthless weight loss programme was when he said to me, looking me straight in the eye, 'Mrs P, I've watched your weight nearly double in the last two years. Your blood pressure has gone up to hazardous levels, you look like you might be developing some blood sugar problems. You're only 53. As your doctor this is hard for me to watch, it's frustrating. I'm seeing you entering dangerous territory. I want to help. Will you let me?'

## Agreeing a next step

Ideally each patient will leave with an agreed action. We humans are simple creatures in many ways. It seems that stating our intention to another person, especially to someone we like and respect, greatly increases the chances that we will do what we say. This agreement also gives you, as the clinician, a good opening line for the next consultation.

This 'next step' has no flavour of parent–child or teacher–pupil interaction but it is still in its mild way asking the patient to be accountable for what they have agreed. If they do it then you can enjoy discussing how well it went, though beware of unintentionally creating that parent–child mode by overdoing the praise. If the patient has relapsed, avoided the action or only partially succeeded, then there will be useful discussion about what got in the way, what did work even if only for a short time, and how to do better next time. This phase of the consultation is best introduced by offering a summary of what you have heard in the consultation. Here is one doctor describing how she did this with a patient whose alcohol consumption was rising steeply. Note how skilfully this doctor mirrors the exact language used by the patient and draws attention to their joint agreement on his current state:

> So, Alex, if I can just summarize what we've discussed today, you are still drinking by our joint reckoning at least 55 units of alcohol a week, mostly lagers. You said this was with 'the lads' after work when you tend to go to the pub every day to wind down because work in your City job is so stressful. At the weekend you avoid alcohol if you can but if there's a party you will go and it's difficult to avoid drinking. You're worried about liver damage and I am too, and about whether you're actually addicted, but the thing you're most worried about is that your girlfriend has threatened to leave you if you don't cut down on booze. She's told you that you get what she calls *boorish* when you're drunk. Is that accurate as a summary?

Assuming that the answer is 'yes', it is usually valuable to then ask the patient to give you a summary of how they see things:

> So tell me what's your current thinking, based on what we've talked through today?

> What are your thoughts and feelings *right now* on when you might start [whatever the healthier behaviour is]?

Then, depending on the reply:

> So what would be a good first step?

> When do you think you might take that step?

> What do you think might get in the way?

> How might you get round that?

> What other information or help do you need from me?

In the example above, there were two immediate steps: the patient was referred at the doctor's suggestion for a comprehensive set of blood tests and a liver scan, and the patient himself suggested, and in his own words, a 'boozer's cold turkey month' which would involve complete abstinence during that time.

## Summary

Patients who present with problems linked to lifestyle choices can lure clinicians into lecturing them or into patronizing them with pity, but a coaching approach is much more likely to be successful. It helps to understand that human beings can be heavily invested in staying stuck and that there are typical stages of readiness as well as pay-offs, familiar excuses and 'discounts' for staying the same. The expert clinician-coach has a flexible range of questions and approaches that will match each phase of the patient's journey to better self-care. A consultation for this type of patient will work best when you move steadily through a process which starts with overtly recognizing that patients must make their own choices, setting goals for each consultation, sticking to the positive whenever possible and agreeing a next step with the patient.

## References

1. Groves, J.E. Taking care of the hateful patient. *New England Journal of Medicine* 1978; 298(16): 883–887
2. Nelson, A., De Normanville, C., Payne, K. and Kelly, M.P. Making every contact count: an evaluation. *Public Health* 2013; 127(7): 653–660.
3. Naqvi, N., Shiv, B. and Bechara, A. The role of emotion in decision-making: a cognitive neuroscience perspective. *Current Directions in Psychological Science* 2006; 15: 260–264.
4. Johnson, F., Beeken, R.J., Croker, H. and Wardle, J. Do weight perceptions among obese adults in Great Britain match clinical perceptions? *BMJ Open* 2014; 4(11): e005561.
5. Jackson, S.E., Beeken, R.J. and Wardle, J. Perceived weight discrimination and changes in weight, waist circumference and weight status. *Obesity* 2014; 22(12): 2485–2488.
6. Graybiel, A.M. Habits, rituals and the evaluative brain. *Annual Review of Neuroscience* 2008; 31: 359–387
7. Ray, D. and Bossaerts, P. Positive temporal dependence of the biological clock implies hyperbolic discounting. *Frontiers in Neuroscience* 2011; 5: 2.
8. Kahneman, D. *Thinking, Fast and Slow*. London: Penguin; 2010.
9. Ariely, D. *Predictably Irrational*. London: HarperCollins; 2009.

10. Peters, G.J.Y., Ruiter, R.A.C. and Kok, G. Threatening communication: a critical re-analysis and a revised meta-analytic test of fear appeal theory. *Health Psychology Review* 2014; 7: S8–31

11. Kringelbach, M.L. and Berridge, K.C. The functional neuroanatomy of pleasure and happiness. *Discovery Medicine* 2010; 9 (49): 579–587.

12. Prochaska, J.O., Norcross, J.C. and DiClemente, C.C. *Changing for Good: The Revolutionary Program that Explains the Six Stages of Change and Teaches You How to Free Yourself from Bad Habits.* New York: W. Morrow; 1994.

13. Adams, J. and White, M. Are activity promotion interventions based on the transtheoretical model effective? A critical review. *British Journal of Sports Medicine* 2003; 37: 106–114.

14. Olson, J.M. Psychological barriers to change. *Canadian Family Physician* 1992; 38: 309–319.

15. Locke, E.A. and Latham, G.P. New directions in goal-setting theory. *Current Directions in Psychological Science* 2006; 15(5): 265–268.

# 5 THE INFORMATION GAME

Giving information is central to virtually every clinical consultation. You will do it in all these situations, and others like them: clarifying the reasons for choosing one type of medication over another, breaking bad news, explaining the health risks involved in smoking or alcohol, demonstrating how to use a piece of equipment, explaining a diagnosis, briefing a patient on what will happen during an operation, seeking informed consent or helping a patient decide between one form of treatment and another. Clinicians know more about health and ill-health than patients do. That simple fact is the foundation of the imbalance of power that gets in the way of using a coaching approach. Doing it badly means that the patient may argue, pay lip service to your ideas or just ignore your suggestions. Doing it well increases the chances that the patient will be an enthusiastic and well-informed partner in their own treatment. In this chapter we look at the critical role of giving information and arriving at decisions – and how to do it in a way which avoids the extremes of either overloading the patient or of oversimplifying.

## Patient anxiety

All clinicians get training in communication. We are taught to avoid jargon, to keep things simple, to offer information in small bites and to double back from time to time to make sure that the patient has understood. It sounds easy. In practice there is so much that can get in the way.

When you are in the patient role, you are acutely aware that the clinician holds information that could literally make the difference between life and death. When you are already made anxious by formless worries, by negative fantasies about what your symptoms could mean, by pain or discomfort, it is all too easy to revert to a child-like state of dependency where your usual confidence deserts you. Anxiety also interferes with thinking power – the brain is less able to process information, and the more panicked you feel the more likely it is that you will not take in what you have been told:

> I began going with my husband to all his appointments at the eye hospital because it was driving me mad to have him come back with such a confused mishmash of messages. When I did go with him, I found it unbearable to see him in these conversations, a faint shadow of his normal assertive self. He told me he felt literally tongue-tied and found it hard to remember anything he had been told, including how much sight he was likely to regain after surgery. When I said this to the surgeon she stared at me in amazement, saying, 'But it's just a routine operation', to which my reply was, 'Yes, routine to you, but not to us!'

> As a doctor myself I was acutely aware of fighting the urge to be submissive when I was diagnosed with acute idiopathic bronchiectasis. Admittedly I was young and junior at the time, but I felt myself slipping into deferential mode and feeling 'just a lad' with the senior chest physician from my own hospital.

> So many long words, so much to take in. When the diagnosis is cancer you feel like a little child again. I wrote myself a list of questions, but I found it difficult to find the courage even to produce the piece of paper let alone to ask the questions.

Whether or not you are anxious as a patient, you may find yourself at a disadvantage:

> I already knew my sarcoma was rare, and when the consultant told me that the biopsy had confirmed the initial diagnosis, I asked what type it was. His immortally condescending reply was, 'You don't need to know that'.

> At the age of only 23 I found myself lying stripped to the waist on a couch while my doctor and a young male trainee were looming over me. I had presented with nipple discharge. After telling me that I was 'too young' to have breast cancer and that it was most probably eczema, while I was still lying there, he and the trainee

had a conversation over me and about me as if I was invisible. 'Yes, it might be Paget's', said the doctor, 'awfully bad luck if it is'. I was appalled and terrified. I was probably the one patient in several hundred who knew that 'Paget's' was a reference to a form of breast cancer. I was speechless, just got dressed and went home.

The orthopaedic surgeon was a nice man and I liked him. I could see he was trying hard to explain, but once he got launched on the types of prosthesis and into cement or no cement, metal on metal, metal on plastic, ceramic on plastic, titanium or ... I was lost. I could see he was a real enthusiast for his craft and he was eager for me to understand, but if he'd stopped just once to ask me how much of it I was following, or even how much I wanted to know all of this detail, it would have made a lot of difference.

## Emotion gets in the way for practitioners, too

Practitioners are not blank sheets, and, however 'professional' you aim to be, emotion will always be present. For instance, pity may get in the way, where the danger is of appearing to oversimplify, wrapping everything up in sympathy and therefore patronizing by assuming that the other person cannot handle whatever information you are offering. If you are anxious yourself and also dealing with an anxious person, the temptation can be to rush through your message, being perfunctory or gabbling and using jargon:

As a neurologist I often have to give patients unwelcome news. It took seeing myself in a videoed consultation to realize that I was beginning with a huge amount of waffle and equivocation, burying the nugget of the message so deep that the patient was unlikely to take it in, talking, talking, talking, lots of long words, because if I'm honest, I was afraid of the patient's reaction and that I couldn't handle it if they broke down or got angry, especially if they got upset with me as the bearer of the news.

Then there may be impatience, boredom, tiredness, feeling unconfident, distracted by issues in your own life. Or it may all just get overfamiliar:

Working as an audiologist you find yourself seemingly having to give the more or less identical information to patients because they fall into recognizable categories: the older person with age-related hearing loss, the parents of a child with perinatally acquired profound sensorineural hearing loss and so on. I find it helps to remind myself all the time that people will have their own unique understanding and needs, otherwise I start droning on with my little model of the human ear to hand, and the danger is that I don't notice that the patient has a glazed look and probably goes away not much the wiser.

Complaints about how information is given or not given are often at the heart of litigation and malpractice suits in healthcare. Disrupted communication is usually the reason why patients so often fail to complete a course of medication, do not return for follow-up appointments or claim that they were never told about side effects and treatment options. In such cases, the clinician will often say indignantly, bruised by the vehemence of the accusations, 'But I did tell them! They just didn't take any notice!' In such cases, we are reminded of the saying that 'the meaning of your communication is the response you get'. In other words, it is too easy to blame the recipient of the message for failing to act on it or understand. The true responsibility lies with the person giving the message.

## It's a relationship

Giving patients information, as with every other aspect of their treatment, is governed by the quality of the relationship. Everything depends on creating and sustaining rapport (see page 47). If you seem not to be listening, to be distracted or in a hurry, you make it unlikely that the patient will take in what you are saying. When information-giving goes wrong, it is almost always because the clinician has forgotten the impact their information can have and has underestimated the need for emotional connection:

> We saw the paediatrician for a routine check up with Cassie. He freaked out when we told him that she isn't standing up or walking yet and not only referred us to a physio but also wants to rush us to a neurologist next week to check her reflexes, telling me she might have cerebral palsy developing as I had forceps and she needed a little bit of oxygen. I tried to tell him my birth wasn't that traumatic and her Apgar was 10 at five minutes, so improved very quickly from the initial 6, but of course he didn't listen to me, talked over me and told me that 6 is very low. I was sick

with worry and it took me a couple of hours to calm down as all I could think about was Cassie in a wheelchair. The paediatrician redeemed himself the next morning by calling to apologize if he had scared me and to say that there were plenty of other reasons this could happen, and he arranged the physio appointment for the next day.

We noticed that our baby son had nystagmus and our family doctor referred us to an eminent consultant ophthalmologist. He had a large retinue of students with him. After a brief examination and with no word to us, this gentleman turned in great excitement to the students crying, 'This baby has albinism!' We were just stunned at his clumsiness, stunned at hearing such devastating news this way.

It is also easy to overlook the possibility that some information-giving may feel like an attack on the patient's competence by concentrating on what is wrong, not on what is going well, as in this example where a young mother describes taking her son for his development check at age 2:

I came away from it feeling humiliated and undermined because it seems I was doing most things wrong: wrong road-safety teaching, wrong sleep patterns, wrong food – including giving him too much milk. She must have repeated five times, 'Milk is a food! Milk is a food!' Not a word of acknowledgement that I was parent to a sociable, charming and well-behaved little boy.

Another reason why information-giving fails is that many clinicians may be tempted to see it as a one-way and not a two-way process, clinging to the idea that information can simply be installed in the patient's head as if it were a piece of software. The reality is that human beings are very poor at absorbing and retaining information given verbally. Not only do the emotional factors get in the way, but also short-term memory declines sharply as we get older: as fast as one piece of information is received it is overwhelmed by the next, making retention difficult.

## The key to it all: information swap

A much better way of looking at the process of providing information is to see it as an information swap, a two-way process where the information the patient gives the clinician is every bit as important as what the clinician offers to the patient. These two examples give a flavour of how impressively smooth and mutually beneficial this can be:

My patient Christina is extraordinary, and yes, we are on first name terms! She has had problems with unstable blood pressure and underlying renal problems for many years, and now that we have found a drug therapy that works reasonably well she still needs monitoring. She always arrives with some anecdote to make me smile and wearing some crazily eccentric piece of clothing. She carries a jazzy-looking notebook, comes highly prepared and I know she will write everything down. We start by establishing her questions and my questions and then working our way through them jointly. Everything is a mutual decision. I don't always feel that these are textbook 'correct' but I absolutely respect her wish to lead her life her way and not mine.

Our little girl was hospitalized as an emergency over Christmas. She needed medication delivered intravenously. The paediatric team were just wonderful. The consultant spent unhurried time greeting Sukie, introducing herself by saying 'I'm Doctor Paula and it's my job to get you feeling fine again'. Then she told her a little joke and got a weak smile in return – she had already stopped crying. Then she held Sukie's hand very tenderly and said, 'I need to give you some medicine that will make you feel better. We do it with one of these in your arm – would you like to hold it? It's a really clever little gadget called a cannula.' Sukie had a good look at it in its sterile packet. Then the paediatrician said, 'Now I'm going to give you some magic cream on your arm – this helps the cannula get busy quickly. OK? Anything you want to ask me?' Sukie asked how it was magic and the consultant smiled and said, 'It tells your arm to let the cannula in!' In no time at all and with no yelling, it was all in place. 'How does it feel?' said the consultant. 'Yucky but OK!' was the reply. 'Mmm, yes, yucky but OK is good'. Then another soft touch on her hand and reassuring stuff to us with the opportunity to ask more questions about what we should look out for and what we thought Sukie needed. We did a lot more of the talking than she did. It was brilliant. I'm sure it was a big part of why Sukie recovered so quickly.

## Offering information in coaching style

The principles that work here are underpinned by a coaching philoso-phy. The patient knows him- or herself and his or her life better than you, as the clinician, ever can. The patient is the one with the power to decide, and the more overtly this is acknowledged in the conversation the better it will be. Whether or not the patient accepts and acts on your information will depend on how skilfully you create a relationship of equals. When you put all this into practice, it leads to a significantly dif-ferent kind of information-giving.

### Being transparent

The first step is to be transparent about what you are doing by telling the patient that you need to give them some information, then pausing.

> I've got your results here and I'd like to explain what they mean. (Pause, looking carefully at the patient.)

> There is some information I need to give you about the best type of diet, what to avoid and what to eat. (Pause.) How does that seem to you?

Here the pause makes it possible for the patient to intervene if they wish.

### Asking permission

The authors of the excellent book, *Motivational Interviewing in Health Care,*[1] make the point that asking permission to give information is like a polite knock on the door. It is asking the patient for their consent to receive whatever you have to tell them. In our view this is more than just a formal gesture: it symbolizes willingness to take the patient's wishes seriously, it honours the principle of their autonomy and also acts as a flag or headline: *I am going to give you some information here, but first I need to check that you are ready to hear it.* Some useful phrases include:

> There's a lot of useful information that I can offer you here, but is it OK to do that now?

> I'd like to make a suggestion here – is that all right by you?

There will be patients who tell you that they would like to hear what you have to say, but that there are other matters on their mind that they would like to deal with first. If so, follow their lead.

People vary hugely in the amount of information they already have. To spare yourself the embarrassment of telling a patient who is an expert on their condition something they already know, it is vital to ask questions that will uncover this:

> I want you to get best value from this discussion, so what do you already know about this?

> Some people have already done a lot of research on their condition – does that include you?

If the answer to the latter question is 'yes':

> So what are your conclusions?

Many patients will have Googled their condition, their drugs or the surgical options. Some clinicians see this as uncomfortably challenging: who is 'right' – the unknown and possibly ludicrously wrong website or the expert (you) sitting in front of the patient? There are more helpful and less helpful ways of dealing with patients who are keen internet researchers:

> Well let's remember that at least 25 per cent of everything medical on the internet is wrong, so I doubt that this will help us.

This implies that the patient is foolish to be interested enough in their own condition to have researched it. It demonstrates a very thin skin on your part. It is highly likely to raise the patient's resistance, mute or expressed openly, to anything further you have to say.

> OK. That's interesting. Did you bring it with you? Can I have a look?

> Yes, I'm familiar with that site, but I wonder if you know this one? [Taps in a name and swivels the screen so that the patient can see]. Shall I print it for you?

This, on the other hand, gives you thinking time. It allows you to assess the quality of the websites, many of which are excellent, and to endorse the information it contains or, if necessary, to suggest alternative websites which are more accurate and helpful. It acknowledges that the patient is a partner who is free to do their own research and, depending on what they have uncovered, that much clinical data is a lot less cut and dried than it may seem.

People also vary in how they like to absorb information, as well as how much of it they want. Ask such questions as:

> Would you like the headlines first and then the detail, or would you like me to go through it step by step?

> Some people like to have all the detail, some prefer to have just a little. Where are you on that?

## Disagreeing

The patient wants an antibiotic prescription; you know it would be useless for what is clearly a viral infection. The patient believes that St John's wort is an alternative to SSRIs for depression; you disagree. You believe that counselling would be the best intervention for a bereaved patient who has asked for antidepressants; but the patient tells you he thinks counselling is 'just a load of rubbish'.

There are innumerable undesirable ways to respond to such situations because none is likely to lead to conclusion where both you and the patient are happy:

- You allow yourself to get angry: you are doing your best and you know what is good for this patient. How dare they contradict you? You try insisting, but the patient fights back, it develops into a bit of an argument and the patient may even complain about you later.
- You hope that the difficulty will go away, timidly attempting some kind of compromise with the patient, but it all feels unsatisfactory somehow.
- You quail before the patient's determination to be in the right, shrug your shoulders and think (or say) 'Well it's up to you', but this leaves you feeling uneasy and guilty. What about your duty of care?

How do you handle situations like this, some of which can be extremely serious?

> My patient was very overweight and had roaringly high blood pressure. She was also experiencing what were likely to be symptoms of cardiac problems. She appeared for appointments almost

weekly but each time resisted my suggestions of tests or medication, telling me that she was a devoted member of her church and that her pastor had promised her 'healing' and that she should put her trust in God, 'not western medicine', i.e. that if she didn't she was being disloyal to him and to her faith. I felt that I was potentially in a wrestling match with the pastor over this lady's life, and annoyed and irritated by what felt like superstition. However, I could see that expressing this was very unlikely indeed to be helpful and also that turning up so often to see me suggested she was more open to help than first appeared. This was my solution: to say to the patient that I honoured her commitment to her faith and that of course it was ultimately her decision, but that her life was in danger. 'Do you think Pastor X would be willing to come in with you, then perhaps we could work together? He would be very welcome.' She looked startled and a little dubious, but said she would ask. She did and he did. This was the first time anyone had ever prayed over a patient in my presence and I joined in with the amens. Then there was a respectful discussion about medication and some investigations – to work alongside laying on of hands from the pastor and the prayers of his congregation. End of problem.

## Learning from outstanding negotiators

Clinicians can learn from decades of research into what differentiates the behaviour of outstanding negotiators and mediators from people who are merely mediocre.[2] This shows that the outstanding negotiators spend far more time listening than talking, that their aim is first to understand the emotion and thinking processes of the other party rather than to push their own point of view because this gives crucial insights into how the other person's mind is working, that they never start with a fixed preference about what should happen and that they are willing to express and take responsibility for their own honest emotion about what is going on in the actual process of negotiating. Translating this into clinical practice, here are some guidelines about dealing with conflicts of opinion between yourself and a patient:

1. First, and vitally important, repress any immediate urge to talk. Listen neutrally and carefully to the patient's views, however much these strike you are misguided, outdated, crackpot or just wrong.

2. Summarize what you have heard the patient say (see also page 66), without giving any clue about your own views.
3. Enquire more into their view, for instance by asking them to say more about the most important aspects of it.
4. Ask about the significance these views have for the patient, for instance, as in the example above, the patient's resistance to medication and tests was about what she perceived to be a test of her faith.
5. Ask permission to offer your own opinion, and then stress the patient's right to disagree, for instance with phrases like 'I'd like to offer you another view here, though I'm aware you may not agree' or 'See what you think of this, but the most recent evidence is …'.
6. Invite the patient to respond, being careful to avoid any feeling that you are pushing them into an argument where they might lose face.
7. If you still disagree, you might say 'So we seem to be at odds here. What do you suggest we do?'.
8. Be prepared at any point to express your own feelings and motivation, for instance: 'I have to say that I'm feeling a bit frustrated here because my own belief is that if you don't have these tests your illness could get worse pretty quickly and I want to help you'.

Here is an example, somewhat compressed in the interests of space, of how using this process can work out in practice:

Elsbet describes herself as 'an ancient hippy' though she is a slim, young-looking 60. She is an enthusiast for alternative therapies of all sorts, including hypnotherapy, homeopathy, acupuncture, reiki and Ayurvedic medicine. She keeps fit with swimming and dancing and has recently become an enthusiast for mindfulness. She avoids antibiotics and takes innumerable supplements. She has been diagnosed with an aggressive form of cancer, has remained impressively calm and has quickly developed a friendly relationship with her oncologist where they are on first name terms.

The difficulty is that her oncologist, Martin, wants her to have a particular form of chemotherapy developed specifically for cancers such as hers. She seems to be committed to a form of alternative treatment which involves an extreme type of diet plus enemas and staying as an in-patient for several weeks in an expensive facility run by XX, one of the companies espousing this treatment, where there would also be massage, 'spiritual healing' and group therapy. After hearing her describe her reluctance to undergo the chemotherapy, Martin asks her to say what she believes the advantages of the alternative approach would be. Elsbet replies using words which Martin recognizes from the website of this organization: *enzymes, toxins, symbiotic, cell renewal, metabolism, mitochondrial, immune system, vitamins, minerals, natural, holistic.*

Martin summarizes skilfully, using Elsbet's words, adding that he agrees with her that food is a critically important part of recovery and that many people underestimate the importance of getting high-quality fruit and vegetables into their diets, that a holistic approach is always helpful and that massage and therapy can be hugely help-ful for patients with cancer. Then he says, 'But I expect you can see some disagreement heading your way. I've had quite a few patients interested in this approach so I've taken time to read the evidence because I'm open to anything that looks promising where cancer is concerned. May I take a few moments to describe my views to you?'

Elsbet interrupts. 'Martin, I know what you're going to say, but people from XX tell me that medical conspiracy with the drug com-panies hides the truth!'

Martin replies, 'Yes, I've read that too and the behaviour of Big Pharma has often been problematical, as we know. But, Elsbet, you haven't answered my question. May I just tell you what my own take is on the evidence?'

Elsbet nods. Very straightforwardly Martin tells her that for her own type of cancer, the available clinical evidence shows there is no viable treatment other than chemotherapy. 'If you don't have it', he says, 'and of course I totally respect your wishes here, you can expect to live for maybe another year. If you have it, your chances of survival for at least 5 years rise to 70 per cent which is good but no doddle, not a guarantee. If it were me or my wife, I would have it. I have to say that I would be very disappointed if you decided against. But it's your choice. Maybe don't give me your answer now. Think about it, call me if you have other questions, you've got my mobile number, and let's get together this time next week because if you want the chemo, it has to start ASAP'.

They part on excellent terms. Elsbet begins the chemotherapy 10 days after this conversation.

In this example, the doctor has suppressed what he later described as 'an overwhelming urge to condemn those idiots as greedy charlatans', has listened with care and respect and starts by agreeing with his patient wherever he can, for instance on the benefits of good diet, therapy, massage and a holistic approach. He stresses her freedom to decide and his concern for her. He deliberately opts for giving her space to decide. He avoids getting into a debate about specific evidence showing that XX, the company Elsbet believes in so passionately, cannot demonstrate any scientifically reliable evidence that they can cure cancer, although he is very familiar with the discourse here. He concentrates instead on a simple, clear message: without the chemotherapy you will most probably die within a year.

## Making decisions

As the example above shows, offering information is often closely linked with asking the patient to make a decision. You may have strong views, as Elsbet's doctor did, on what that decision should be. The danger is of pushing your view on the basis of clinical data alone, without knowing where the decision fits with the patient's values and beliefs or with what else is going on in their lives. Our experience of training clinicians is that they often make a good job of explaining the options but are less confident about exploring them with the patient. Where this happens clumsily – or not at all – it diminishes the chances of getting to a mutually agreed management plan.

The scene in this example is a dental surgery where a 35-year-old patient has presented with a painful infection. Examination reveals that he has extensive problems in all four front upper teeth, including excessive mobility, periodontal disease, discoloration which is affecting his smile, and that the four teeth need to be extracted. There are further problems with the adjacent teeth.

### Scenario 1

The dentist takes time to explain the problem with the teeth and outlines two possibilities, dentures and implants, emphasizing that the status quo is not an option. The patient asks a few questions and then asks about cost; the dentist gives him estimates. The patient explains that he has a chronic fear of dental surgery which is why he has allowed his teeth to get to their current state. The dentist reassures him that modern dentistry is pain-free. The patient leaves and never returns.

## Scenario 2

The dentist takes time to explain the problem with the teeth and outlines two possibilities, dentures and implants, emphasizing that the status quo is not an option. The patient asks a few questions and then asks about cost; the dentist gives him estimates.

The dentist says, 'So these are the possibilities. How do they strike you?

The patient hesitates. 'Don't know – worried!'

The dentist asks, 'What worries you specifically?'

'I had an abscess as a teenager then had to have some of my teeth taken out and I was aware of the pain all the time, it was horrible. The dentist also told me off for eating sugary food and fizzy drinks and I've avoided dentists ever since.'

The dentist listens quietly, expresses empathy and comments that this happened twenty years ago and that dentistry and dentists have come a long way since then. He explains that modern dentistry is reliably pain-free most of the time and that he is used to helping very nervous patients with sedation if necessary and can also offer hypnosis, which benefits many patients. He notices that the patient now looks a lot less stressed.

The conversation turns to the treatment options. The dentist asks, 'So tell me how you will judge which of these treatments is going to be best for you. What really matters to you?'

The patient plunges in with a lot of information. He is an actor, he only finds work sporadically and has little money. He has debts, his credit rating is poor and he doubts that he can borrow money. It really matters to him how he looks because it is how he gets jobs. He has memories of his granddad with poorly fitting dentures that clacked when he talked. He'd like to have implants but he dreads the intrusive nature of the treatment and in any case can't afford the much higher cost.

'So if you had to rate these factors, which of them is the priority for you?

The patient pauses. 'Money first, then getting a result that won't embarrass me when I smile, then no pain!'

There is a further brief discussion, where the dentist offers reassuring information about how modern dentures work, then pauses and says, 'So, to summarize, cost is the critical factor for you, then appearance, practicality and pain-free treatment. Of the options we've discussed, which appeals to you most?'

The patient's reply is swift. He agrees to the extractions, opts for dentures, saying that if his acting career takes off he will return for implants at a later date. The treatment is successful. The patient's confidence is hugely boosted and his career as an actor takes a turn for the better.

In the second scenario, the clinician realizes that the decision will be made on criteria that matter to the patient and that his role as a clinician is to draw these out. Making these criteria explicit will virtually always mean that decision-making is significantly quicker and easier.

## Calibrating the flow of information

Despite what we learn during our training, evidence[3] suggests that clinicians do most of the talking in a consultation, typically interrupting a patient within 20 seconds. The overwhelming urge is to pass on to patients what we believe they should know. The typical pattern is to give information in downloading style where large chunks of talking from the clinician are interspersed by brief closed questions. The practitioner talks for several minutes, ending with a closed question which expects the answer 'yes': 'Do you understand?' The patient answers 'yes', as he or she knows is expected. The practitioner talks for several more minutes, ending with another closed question: 'Anything else you want to know?' The patient understands that this is intended to bring the consultation to a close and replies, 'No, thanks'.

Although there might be occasions where this 'telling' style is effective, mostly it will not be. The patient has limited chances to process the information, to bring up reservations, to ask for clarification or to ask for more information. When this style of telling is combined with the feeling that as the patient you are being instructed on what to do by a more evolved human being, your resistance is raised, reducing the likelihood of following whatever advice you have been given, including whether you adhere to prescribed medication.

## The drawing-out-then-adding approach

A better and more powerful approach is to create an informal setting where you start by drawing out what the patient knows, offer a small slice of information, create space for the patient to disagree, ask questions, offer their own take on what seems possible for them, and then follow flexibly with more questions and information-offering. This type of consultation has the flavour of a conversational dance rather than, as so many do, of a lecture. This is how it might go:

| | | |
|---|---|---|
| Practitioner | I'd like to make a suggestion here. Is that OK by you? | *Asking permission with a closed question expecting the answer 'yes'* |
| Patient | Says yes. | |
| Practitioner | May start by asking what the patient already knows, or by offering a short chunk of information ending with 'But I'd like to know how that strikes you'. | *Gives patient the chance to state an initial response, for instance to ask a question* |
| Patient | May express a reservation about how well it fits with their life and needs. | *Gives practitioner vital information and the chance to modify the next chunk of information* |
| Practitioner | Asks the patient to say more about their reservation. | *Listening with respect to reservations dismantles resistance* |
| Patient | Explains their doubts or offers their own ideas. | |
| Practitioner | Summarizes what the patient has said. | *Shows the patient they have been heard* |
| Practitioner | Goes on to the next chunk of information, adapting what they say to what they have heard, using the same approach of keeping it brief followed by stopping for patient input. | |

It may seem as if this will take longer, and it may – perhaps a minute or so, but in the longer term less time will be involved as each subsequent consultation is likely to be based a high level of trust and to get to the heart of the problems more quickly.

## Emphasizing autonomy

We suggested in Chapter 2 that autonomy is an essential human need. The more you stress the patient's autonomy, the more likely it is that you will find solutions that meet both your own and the patient's needs. One way to do this is being explicit about offering choices and then ending with a question. Here are some examples:

> There are lots of ways of reintroducing exercise that would be equally good, for instance a 20 minute brisk walk every day, swimming 15 lengths, going to a dance class. Ideally it needs to be something you really enjoy. You'll probably be able to think of similar things. How much do any of those appeal?

> It's very common to find it difficult to cope with anxiety, but apart from pills, some other things that work for many people are getting some regular exercise – enough to raise your heart rate, writing down how you feel in a little notebook, talking to a counsellor. What do you feel about those as ideas?

You can boost the impact of these suggestions by giving brief anecdotes from the experience of other patients. Research from social psychology[4] shows how much we are affected by other people's experience and by the human urge to be part of the herd. Which of these statements would be likely to affect you more?

(a) 10 per cent of patients report side effects with this medication.
(b) 90 per cent of patients had no side effects with this medication.

The statistics are exactly the same, but the chances are that you would find option (b) more persuasive because it what 'most people' experience as well as being a more optimistic message. Adding some mini-anecdotes to your suggestions will increase their persuasiveness:

> A practitioner specializing in smoking cessation offers the patient, now clearly ready to give up, three anecdotes:

I'm going to give you some examples of what other people in your situation have done. I've worked for ten years now with people who are on the way to becoming non-smokers, and what works for one person will not necessarily work for another. So I worked with someone recently who had been a really heavy smoker for 40 years and he found that stopping altogether on a day he announced in advance was the best for him – and it worked because he'd told so many people and got a lot of support from his friends and family. Another person, this was someone in her twenties, went for two hypnosis sessions and even though she was really dubious about it, it did the trick. And a good friend of mine who had just got pregnant felt she couldn't give up straight off but she steadily cut down with one less cigarette every other day until she was down to zero. I thought that was the hard way to do it, but she said it was fine and she's still a non-smoker. I can tell you about other people as well, but what do you think?

## Expressing doubts and uncertainty

It can be tempting for clinicians to express certainty and for patients to want to be offered it, whereas the reality is that there are many situations where there is ambiguity. No one can say exactly how any particular patient will respond to a treatment, exactly how long someone might live or how a particular illness will affect the overall quality of life of a patient. Some clinicians will claim that patients like certainty because in a stressful situation it is helpful to be guided by someone who is clear and focused. Only you can assess what degree of certainty any one patient needs. Part of the way to find out is to ask questions such as 'What kind of detail do you want to have about your illness/treatment/medication?', and to be guided by the patient's answer.

The more committed you are to treating patients as partners in the management of their conditions, the more likely you are to err on the side of honesty about doubts and dilemmas. Many patients will appreciate it, especially when there is no easy or obvious way forward:

> My husband, Tom, was admitted with a shoulder fracture. He was already a 'difficult' case as he was in a wheelchair after failed hip

surgeries, very unfit and overweight as a result, had broken his neck some years earlier, so intubating him was challenging. The question was whether surgery would help. I was deeply impressed that the doctor who did the initial assessment introduced himself as Andrew X, so not 'Dr X', examined him, listened carefully to his story, sat down at Tom's bedside rather than standing over him and then said, 'Tom, I'm not sure what the best thing to do is here, I need to talk to my senior'. He came back 30 minutes later with more information and set out the various options, pausing unhurriedly for Tom's input at each stage. He emphasized that there was no obvious or ideal solution. It felt like an entirely right thing that we all agreed eventually that doing nothing was the safest route, even though we all knew and had discussed exactly what disadvantages that would mean.

## This is not coaching

Some clinicians understand importance of patient autonomy, but they misjudge how to use it:

> James is a 58-year-old diagnosed with a stage 1 cancer of the prostate. He returns from a consultation at his local hospital trembling with anger and worry. 'This doctor told me bluntly that I had cancer and that it was at an early stage. He just fired off a few questions and told me it was up to me whether I wanted to have surgery or this drug for a few months. How was I to know? He handed me a bundle of leaflets. He said to make an appointment when I'd decided and to talk to my family doctor first. Then he rushed off. But how could I decide? I'm not a doctor!'

In this case the clinician has grasped that James needs to feel involved in his treatment. He has probably accepted that patients have strong feelings about surgery and about side effects from drugs. Possibly there is nothing much to choose between the options he has offered in terms of clinical outcome. But he has missed the opportunity and reneged on the duty to coach James on what each treatment would involve and how likely each might be to offer a long-term cure, let alone to explore what his feelings are about the diagnosis. Instead of feeling empowered, James feels abandoned.

## The language of optimism

The overall aim of any clinical interaction is that the patient leaves feeling capable of managing their own condition, experiencing hope and optimism. Even where the prognosis is grim, it is possible for the patient to leave feeling able to manage their life. It is easy to underestimate the immense importance of the language you use in making sure that this is what happens (see also page 63).

There is now a mass of research showing that the human brain is fine-tuned to respond viscerally to words, especially in the heightened emotion of a health crisis.[5] The autonomic nervous system kicks in at an unconscious level and out of our immediate control. We are enormously suggestible, especially where pain is involved. This explains both the placebo and the 'nocebo' effects. The nocebo effect is where no actual treatment is given but the patient believes it has and describes negative effects. The well-meant phrase 'This may hurt, but only a bit' will often have the effect of increasing the amount of pain the patient experiences because the brain hears the powerful word *hurt* and discounts the softening words *may* and *only a bit*. A better phrase might be 'This might tingle for a moment but most people find they barely notice it'. Similarly, the phrase 'don't worry' conveys the message that there is something to worry about.

There is a fine art in carefully choosing words to programme the brain towards minimal pain and maximum healing. For instance, never underestimate how important it is to use phrases which normalize the patient's condition and predict a positive outcome – and to avoid the phrases which express doubt. So the word *try* is a failure word, it suggests that disappointment is possible, as in 'We will *try* to manage this condition with drugs'. A future-focus which implies success is much more helpful. There is world of difference in 'You *may* find this will solve the problem' and 'Most patients find that this solves the problem'.

Some of the everyday language of clinicians has considerable potential to dismay patients. For instance, talking about a 'trapped nerve' may suggest that only surgery can untrap it. A 'frozen' shoulder sounds permanently solid: 'stiff' would be a better word. 'Degeneration' sounds like disintegration and may alarm a patient into believing that their entire body is crumbling, whereas 'wear and tear' is a lot less disturbing.

Here are some other examples:

| Phrases with potential to alarm | Optimistic alternatives |
|---|---|
| (Anaesthetist) I will put you to sleep [May remind the patient of euthanizing a pet] | You will be asleep during the operation and when you wake up it will all be fine |
| The wound will hurt like hell for a bit | That tight itchy feeling is a good sign that the wound is healing |
| This [antacid] may make you feel sick for a little while [increases likelihood that patient will vomit] | This will protect your stomach |
| The craving for nicotine is very strong – I know it's difficult to resist [emphasizes the difficulty] | Most people find when they're giving up that the craving for nicotine only actually lasts for a few seconds and it's easier than they thought to ignore it |
| Sciatica is an excruciating pain but we'll do our best to help you through it [the patient will hear the drama of 'excruciating pain', while 'do our best' suggests that success is not very likely] | For 90 per cent of patients sciatica is a relatively short-lived problem – it resolves itself as a rule [then describes short-term pain management] |
| It's essential to avoid another fracture and of course if you sit around all day and don't exercise you'll make that more likely [Combines threat with negative words]. | Pilates and yoga are good for building strength and flexibility and a generous amount of walking will build up strength in your bones, reducing the risk of fracture. |

## The healing power of language

Calming, positive words before, during and after surgery also have the potential to speed recovery.[6] Here are two examples of seamlessly well-handled patient experiences:

It was three hours of complex dental surgery and I was very apprehensive about the sedation, a new experience for me. Would I do or say something daft? Was it true that I would not experience pain? In cheerfully answering all my questions and describing it all to me, I noticed that the dental surgeon and anaesthetist both avoided using the word 'pain' at all. Instead they used phrases like, 'Most people say it's a very pleasant experience', 'You will be able to respond to instructions but you won't feel anything', 'The time will pass in what will feel like seconds, you won't really remember any of it and you'll be amazed when you look at the clock'. I was very dimly aware during the procedure of hearing things like, 'This is going well'. Afterwards it was phrases like, 'It looks good and it will heal up very quickly', then a little later when I'd come round properly, 'I'll give you some tablets just in case you get some discomfort, but I don't think you'll need them'. And so it was. No pain during the surgery, no pain afterwards, no infection, rapid healing'.

The X-ray showed that the fractured scaphoid had healed, the plaster had come off but the hand felt so weak, I was afraid of using it despite having been told to 'mobilize it' without any explanation of how to do this and the promised hand therapy had not materialized. So I went to an osteopath. He did some massage and manipulation but he then held and gently addressed the hand specifically: 'Poor little hand, you've had a shock but you're fine now, you've healed, you are strong again'. I left able to grip things and turn the hand far more effectively. The funny thing was, I was perfectly aware of the 'technique' but it worked like the magic maybe it was!'

We end this chapter with the words of the writer and surgeon Atul Gawande from his third BBC Reith Lecture[7] given in 2014:

But the way that people come to grips with their anxieties is not by hearing facts but instead by saying the truth for themselves, by putting it into their own words. And so when I asked folks as I interviewed them, I'd say 'So what would be on the checklist you would give me to use in my next office visit when I come to a critical decision point with a patient about whether we should do an operation or not or other kinds of considerations?' And one of the items that people said I ought to have on my list is that in that conversation I should be talking less than 50 per cent of the time while we're in that room. And so I paid attention to what I was doing in those conversations and to my horror I found I was talking 90 per cent of the time. I had lots of facts and figures and pros and cons and risks and benefits, so now what do you want to do? And I'd see this bewildered person across from me.

They also said you know if you are going to talk less than 50 per cent of the time, the key thing is you have to be able to ask questions. And there are certain questions that I saw people ask that were really great at eliciting what people's real understanding and their priorities were. The first question was to ask, 'What is your understanding of where you are with your condition or your illness at this time?'

## Summary

Giving patients information in coaching style means creating a conversational exchange where you share the talking equally. Apparently small behaviours such as asking questions to uncover what the patient already knows, creating space for questions, seeing disagreements as opportunities for negotiation and keeping to positive language can all have major impact on reaching a place where clinician and patient are each happy with the outcome.

## References

1. Rollnick, S, Miller, W.R. and Butler, C.C. *Motivational Interviewing in Healthcare.* New York: Guilford Press; 2008.
2. Olekalns, W. and Adair, W.L. *Handbook of Research on Negotiation.* Cheltenham: Edward Elgar; 2013.
3. Beckman, H.B. and Frankel, R.M. The effect of physician behavior on the collection of data. *Annals of Internal Medicine* 1984; 101: 692–696.
4. Gladwell, M. *The Tipping Point: How Little Things Can Make a Big Difference.* New York: Little, Brown; 2000.
5. Lang, P.J., Bradley, M.M. and Cuthbert, B.N. Emotion, motivation, and anxiety: brain mechanisms and psychophysiology. *Biological Psychiatry* 1998; 44(12): 1248–1263.
6. Kekecs, Z. and Varga, K. Positive suggestion techniques in somatic medicine: A review of the empirical studies. *Interventional Medicine & Applied Science* 2013; 5(3): 101–111.
7. Gawande, A. Why do doctors fail? Reith Lectures 2014: The Future of Medicine, Boston, 2014. http://downloads.bbc.co.uk/radio4/open-book/2014_reith_lecture3_edinburgh.pdf (accessed 19 August 2015).

# 6 IN IT FOR THE LONG TERM

Our population is ageing, our lifestyle and habits are changing. Increasing numbers of people are living with chronic long-term conditions such as asthma, diabetes, coronary heart disease, hypertension, depression, glaucoma, chronic kidney disease, or other long-term health conditions and disabilities such as dementia, for which there is currently no cure. This means a massive commitment of healthcare resources.[1] Despite this, around 80–90 per cent of care is carried out by the patients themselves or by their families. *Multimorbidity*, the state of having more than one chronic condition at the same time, adds to the challenge of managing these patients, and we know from research[2] that patients with multimorbidities are also more likely to experience being socially marginalized, with higher levels of poverty and more mental illness. This chapter explores how coaching approaches to health for these patients are being successfully implemented, drawing on the principles we describe earlier in this book.

There is increasing evidence[3,4] that supporting patients with long-term conditions in the skills of managing their own health can greatly improve the quality of their lives and that clinical outcomes are strikingly better. Patients who have a high level of *activation* – in other words, who have the skills and confidence to play a leading role in managing their own conditions – do experience better quality of life and improved health outcomes.[5]

Liza is a 69-year-old widow with long-standing hypertension. She works part-time as a personal trainer and dance teacher. She lived in France for many years, only returning to the UK because her younger daughter was struggling as a single parent to manage a child with a severe form of autism. She reports finding British doctors 'nannyish and controlling' compared with her experience in France. After much research, she has found a primary care physician whom she likes and who, she says, 'will treat me as an adult and refrain from giving me daft lectures on exercise and diet when I probably know more about that than they do'. Liza experiences 'white coat hypertension', that is her blood pressure soars if taken by a doctor. She avers that this would encourage any clinician to overtreat her. The reason she likes her current primary care physician is that he trusts her to take her blood pressure regularly at home using a high-quality monitor. She had done this in France, reporting the results regularly and jointly reviewing her medication, on which she has made herself well informed. Result: stable blood pressure and a patient who makes minimal demands on local services.

When Peter was diagnosed with Parkinson's disease, he felt devastated. 'How was I going to manage myself? I felt ashamed, I felt like hiding away.' But thanks to an innovative local self-management and coaching programme for Parkinson's patients and their families, Peter is doing well. 'It was only six meetings but it was brilliant. My wife came with me. We met other people with PD. There was a physio, a neurologist, etc., but they stressed that we were the experts. I learnt about exercise, posture and movement control, how to deal with those annoying people who insist on suggesting quack 'cures'. I also learnt how to explain it to people and to handle stares, and actually, thanks to a conversation with the physio, enrolled for Pilates, which has been amazing; learnt about medication and previously had been totally confused about *dopamine replacement*, *copycats*, *protectors* etc., but now I know what they each do. I know it's not going to go away, but I feel so much more confidence and so does my wife.'

Fran's crippling aches and pains were finally and to her great relief given a name: lupus. She is an enthusiast for knowing everything there is to know about how to manage it herself, but she singles out her hospital consultant for special praise: 'She discusses everything with me. When I said that the tramadol made me feel sick all the time and on one of the other drugs I was constipated and felt half dead – and had stopped taking them despite the pain – she suggested an alternative. She asked me about my life in a lovely way that didn't make me feel silly and I was able to confess my lack of exercise and asked me about what I'd always wanted to do where exercise was concerned. "Learn to swim", was the answer. A few days later I enrolled for lessons at the local pool with my wonderful teacher Annie, and I've been going ever since plus two extra visits where I practise. I still get tired and miserable when I have what I call *spiky days*, but I feel I'm in control and that lupus isn't controlling me.'

Terence is a former farm worker in his late eighties. He is a survivor of three heart attacks, has had major cardiac surgery and lives alone. As well as cardiac problems, he has moderate hearing loss and osteoarthritis. He has nothing but praise for the local hospital and for his primary care physician. 'They've sat me down and let me say what mattered to me. The best bit was my first session after my last heart attack when the consultant sat at my bedside and said, "Now Mr James, talk me through your typical day because I want to understand what it's like to be you so that we can work out together what will best keep you going".' Terence was also impressed by the consultant's interest in his 17-year-old analogue hearing aids. These were too uncomfortable to wear for long and did not work well. As Terence explained to the consultant, he did not feel he could justify asking for new ones 'at my age' despite being aware that deafness was adding to his sense of isolation. A letter to Terence's primary care physician triggered an appointment with an audiologist whose view was that the aids needed to be put into a museum of hearing aid horrors. Terence now walks three miles every day, has joined a bowls club and, much to the amusement of his neighbours, does t'ai chi in his garden every morning along with two equally elderly friends from the bowls club. His discreet new digital hearing aids mean that he can communicate without embarrassment, his loneliness has abated and his cardiac condition has stabilized.

Despite these success stories and hundreds of others like them, the management of patients with long-term conditions is often still fragmented, disease-focused and reactive.[6] A priority for healthcare systems around the world is to improve the care of patients with long-term conditions through a shift to a preventative, holistic and proactive approach, enabling them to managing their conditions more effectively, improving physical and emotional well-being and changing the way these patients use services.

Managing patients with long-term conditions, including those with multimorbidities, needs a different approach from those that are appropriate for acute conditions which are likely to resolve with time. It is vital that these patients are empowered and supported to take on a self-management role confidently, and this has been increasingly recognized by healthcare commissioners, providers and decision-makers. In 2014, the Royal College of General Practitioners published the results of their *Inquiry into Patient Centred Care in the 21st Century*.[7] They described three core, interrelated aspects of patient-centred care:

- a holistic (or whole-person) approach;
- flexible care that tailors support according to an individual's personal priorities, needs and individually defined outcomes;
- the need for a collaborative approach between patients and the professionals involved in caring for them, empowering patients to be equal partners in their own care.

This description fits seamlessly with the principles of health coaching described in Chapter 2, providing further strong endorsement of the idea that the time has come for a health coaching approach to become the norm in healthcare consultations, placing genuinely patient-centred care firmly at the heart of the process.

## The importance of taking a whole-life view

Barbara has a history of hypertension and has not been collecting her prescriptions for some months. She has also been diagnosed with depression for which she is on medication which she does appear to be taking. She was offered counselling but has not attended. It is a year since her blood pressure has been measured. The trap for a practitioner would be to ask a series of *why* questions, all of which would put the patient on the defensive. *Why* haven't you taken advantage of the counselling we're offering you? *Why* haven't you collected your prescriptions for four months? *Why* haven't you come in for your blood pressure check?

Instead, as the patient comes in, a new physician, Sara, smiles and introduces herself, before asking 'What brings you here today?'

Barbara pours out her story, while Sara listens attentively and without interrupting. She says she is not coping at home. She discloses that she has three young children. The eldest has cerebral palsy and attends a school for children with special needs. She is a single mother. She says that her husband left when he could not cope with the demands of a child needing such high levels of care, and she has little in the way of other family or social support. Her son's behaviour at home is getting worse, but she is feeling so low and isolated that she does not feel able to have productive conversations with her son's school or key worker and does not know where to turn. 'I know I should have gone for the counselling and come here for my blood pressure check, but honestly I haven't had the energy.'

'That sounds tough', says Sara, leaving a pause for Barbara to nod. After a brief summary, she says, 'Let's try something different here. It sounds as if the biggest problem is your feeling that you're coping alone. Let's imagine you have all the help you need. Where would you get that? Could we make a list here and now?'

Using paper and pen, they then brainstorm a list of all the sources of support available for her son. Sara then asks if there is anything else she would like to add to the list. Barbara thinks carefully before replying, 'Yes, I'd like to add myself to the list'.

'Which of these places and people are the most important sources of support? Which ones do you feel you have most control over?'

After another pause, Barbara takes the pen and circles herself on the paper. This exploration has helped her to realize that to be of most use to her son, she needs to be in good health physically and emotionally.

'So what needs to happen, do you think, for that to happen?' asks Sara, smiling as she notices that Barbara is also smiling.

'I think you need to check my blood pressure now and I think I need to take my pills. And maybe if I feel a bit better I might think about the counselling – or maybe I won't need it!'

Over the coming weeks and months, Barbara attends for all her appointments and collects her prescriptions regularly. She reports feeling more in control of her health, more confident, better able to liaise with her son's school and key worker and more motivated to access the help on offer.

A point sometimes made by participants on our courses is that there are patients who just need to be told what to do and warned about the consequences to their health of not following advice. The example above illustrates that the patient did not need a lecture about the importance of controlling her hypertension or depression: it would not have worked because other factors in her life had assumed far greater importance. The answer in this case was to work with the patient's agenda, tapping into her own resourcefulness through using a coaching approach, supporting her in finding her own solutions. Regaining energy to deal with her life problems then had a positive impact on her health issues.

## A 'situational' approach to working with patients

Matt Driver is an executive coach, writer and colleague who has worked closely with us to develop and deliver coach training sessions for doctors and other healthcare professionals. Through his interest in leadership he has made a useful connection[8] between coaching for health and the Hersey and Blanchard *situational leadership* model,[9] originally developed to train managers. This model is based on adapting your leadership style, depending on the levels of competence and motivation of those being led. In our version, the model sees clinical interaction with the patient categorized along one axis according to the level of intensity the clinician needs to bring to the relationship, and along the other axis the level of guidance you perceive the patient to need (Figure 6.1). This in its turn will depend on your judgement about the patient's levels of commitment and capacity at the time. There are four quadrants:

- telling,
- selling,
- coaching/participation,
- delegating.

The model is dynamic, so a patient may move through each of the four quadrants during the time you are involved in their care, starting with a nervous patient who needs an emphasis on telling, through

| High | | |
|---|---|---|
| **Intensity of clinician relationship with patient** | **3. Coaching/participation**<br><br>Patient well motivated, well informed, and a coaching approach will support and empower them to identify and work towards achieving their health-related goals | **2. Selling**<br><br>Patient may be dubious, still uncommitted or not well informed; needs information and discussion but given in friendly two-way style, adult to adult |
| | **4. Delegating**<br><br>Patient largely self-managing and self-monitoring with light-touch clinician overview and review | **1. Telling**<br><br>Emergency situations or those where patient lacks capacity or confidence to make own decisions |
| Low | **Level of clinician guidance** | High |

**Figure 6.1** The situational model of health coaching

to selling as your preferred style as they grow in confidence but still need persuasion, then coaching where they are learning how to self-manage their conditions, and, finally, delegating where they know when to report new symptoms and how to monitor a condition themselves.

## Telling

Sometimes a telling approach is the correct one, as in the following example:

Alan is a 60-year-old businessman whose health problems started with juvenile arthritis diagnosed when he was a teenager. Ankylosing spondylitis followed, then chronic lymphoedema and the loss of sight in one eye. He has had five hip replacements and has severely limited mobility, but this does not prevent him working full-time as managing director of his company. He has now been admitted to hospital as an emergency with a third episode of the serious soft tissue infection, cellulitis. Septicaemia has been diagnosed.

Alan is a cheerful, friendly, articulate and well-informed patient. He has insisted on first name terms with all of the many clinicians he has encountered through a lifetime of complex health issues, whether doctors, nurses, physiotherapists, pharmacists or radiographers. He enjoys discussing research on medication or the subtleties of surgery with his doctors and has been known to tease them with challenging questions. Now he is in intensive care with a high temperature and incipient kidney failure. He has been unable to pass urine for several hours and has had mild hallucinations. He has developed an acute confusional state secondary to kidney failure. Simon, the consultant intensivist proposes dialysis. Alan immediately resists:

'No, I really don't want that, I'll be fine, I've been like this before, just give me time and I'll be able to pee.'

'Alan,' says Simon, 'your kidneys are packing up, you haven't been like this before and we're running out of time.'

'I have been like this before, I'll be fine, honest, don't bully me. Simon', says Alan, giving him a wink.

Simon makes a formal assessment that Alan does not have the capacity currently to consent to the dialysis treatment he needs as he is unable to understand or retain the information required to make a decision, and therefore unable to use that information to make a decision. He communicates this to Alan's wife who understands and supports Simon's decision to start Alan on dialysis.

Simon speaks crisply and warmly, 'Alan, this isn't bullying. Kidney problems lead to a degree of mental confusion. I know you usually know best, but this time you don't. I'm overruling you. Your life is in danger. You are having dialysis. It probably won't be for long, just till we get everything working again and give those IV antibiotics a chance to do their job.'

Alan knows when he is beaten. He gives in gracefully – this time.

This example meets all the criteria for adopting a telling approach. The clinician can see that the patient, normally a high-functioning, competent man, has temporarily lost his capacity to consent to treatment because he is in an acute confusional state. There is compelling evidence that it is an emergency. The clinician does know best. There is no time or case for detailed explaining, persuading or joint decision-making. The clinician has to make the decision in the best interests of his patient.

However, the majority of healthcare interactions with patients do not meet the criteria for a telling approach. Nevertheless, it is often the one that clinicians use as their default, as in this example:

> Shilpa is a 65-year-old Indian patient at a large primary care practice. She has poorly controlled diabetes. She dutifully attends for her blood test appointment.
>
> Shilpa feels uneasy. She has not been sticking to the lifestyle changes she promised she would make last time, and is frightened that she will be scolded about her blood test results, knowing that she cannot hide behind the numbers.
>
> She misses the appointment, telling her family that she 'forgot'. The practice sends her a reminder letter. She likes and trusts her usual doctor but he is on holiday and she sees a doctor she has never met before. He is shocked by her blood test results. Privately he believes that patients need what he calls 'wake-up calls' and that fear will motivate them. As a fit young man who loves exercise, he cannot understand why patients will not do the sensible thing, so he literally wags a finger at her, saying that that her blood test shows a worsening of blood sugar levels, reiterating that she must change her diet, do more exercise, lose weight and take her medication properly.
>
> Shilpa avoids his gaze and stays silent as he warms to his little homily. She feels ashamed and embarrassed. She backs out of the room apologetically, promising earnestly that she will try much harder this time, but based on her previous behaviour, the chances that this will happen are extremely slim. In fact you should note (see also page 114) that any patient who says they will 'try' is more or less telling you that they know they are making a promise they cannot keep.

## Selling

At a practice meeting, someone raises the question of patients with diabetes who do not keep to the recommended regime. Shilpa gets a mention as an example. The selling approach is the one most likely to work with her as it seems clear that she is still uncommitted to her treatment.

'I don't think threats work', says her usual doctor, now back from holiday, and he glances at the specialist nurse, knowing that she has high-level skills with such patients.

Later that day, Shilpa gets a phone call.

'Hello, it's Janette, the nurse from the practice. How are you?'

Before she knows it, Shilpa has agreed to an unhurried appointment with Janette.

It's a comfortable room with soft seating as well as the normal clinical furniture and equipment. Janette greets her patient warmly and begins by suggesting that they jointly review how Shilpa is feeling. 'Not too good' is the reply. She has an elderly mother-in-law to visit daily, a husband to look after and two adult children still at home. She feels jaded, is tired all the time, ashamed about being so overweight and worried about the diabetes. She reveals that she has a number of social commitments where, as a talented cook, she is in charge of providing the food. This is invariably Asian, often deep-fried using ingredients such as clarified butter. She makes delicious and complicated desserts for these events and gets to enjoy the leftovers. Finding time for exercise or for a different type of cooking, she believes, would be horribly disruptive to her current way of organizing her life.

'Mmm', says Janette, carefully choosing a closed question, 'So it would be good to have more energy to deal with what sounds like a lot of responsibility?'

After a few more minutes of discussion during which Janette builds the patient's awareness of her own dissatisfaction (fatigue, worry), she is poised to move to the next stage. 'How much do you know about diabetes?'

By creating a friendly, non-judgemental environment, Janette has made it possible to confess to ignorance. Very shyly and tentatively, Shilpa begins to reveal how little she knows and to ask all the questions that most of the clinicians who have met Shilpa previously would probably believe they had already answered. But this patient had been too anxious to take in much, if any, of it. She did not truly understand the causes of Type 2 diabetes, nor its long-term consequences, nor that it was a progressive disease, nor that its deadly development could be significantly slowed by exercise, diet and medication. Shilpa now asks a number of sensible questions. How much and what type of exercise will make a difference? What is the link with her eye problems and hypertension? What happens if she forgets to take her medication for a day? She is nervous about every single aspect of injecting insulin and monitoring glucose, so nervous that it seems easier not to bother.

Sitting now side by side, Janette patiently talks Shilpa through the whole protocol, starting with using the glucose testing kit and going on to injecting. At each stage, Shilpa carries out the procedure herself, with Janette checking that she has got it right. Then there is a discussion about how useful glucose monitoring is because it can show how well the insulin is working. To recap, Janette uses her tablet to play Shilpa a short video and scribbles the reference on the leaflet that her patient will take away with her, knowing that one of her sons will be able to show her how to access it on his phone.

Finally, Janette says, 'Let's just review how far we've got today. How has this been for you?'

Shilpa says politely that it has been good. She has learnt a lot.

'How far do you think you'll be able to do this at home?'

There is a lengthy pause. 'Not sure, it's a lot to take in.'

Janette hides any disappointment she may be feeling and says brightly, 'Let's meet again in a week. Then we can go through it all again. Also, there's a half day workshop I'd like you to go to. It's run by a local diabetes charity and you'd meet a lot of other people in the same boat – most of my patients say they really enjoy the day.'

## Coaching/participating

Janette is confident that Shilpa will attend the follow-up meeting, and she does. Shilpa will probably be ready for a coaching approach where she is committed, knows the essential principles of what to do, but has some further questions and will benefit from support and encouragement.

Janette starts by agreeing some goals for the consultation. 'I'm eager to know how you've got on with what we agreed last time, but what do you need from me today?'

The answer is that Shilpa would like to ask some more questions about glucose monitoring. She has surprised herself by getting on well with it, saying it was easier to do than she had thought. She has discovered some interesting trends in her glucose levels, seeing for herself what impact it has to eat certain foods and in what quantities. Janette nods, noticing that Shilpa is doing most of the talking this time. Shilpa asks how frequently she should use the monitor. Rather than reply with advice, Janette asks her what her own answer would be and, when she gets it, says, 'Yes, that sounds right to me'. Janette also mentions a diabetes charity helpline and their high-quality website, showing it to Shilpa and writing down the website address for her.

Now the discussion turns to lifestyle. In answer to Janette's neutrally put question, Shilpa suggests that she could easily put into place simple changes like adjusting the quantities of the food she cooks, and freezing or offering any leftovers to friends rather than eating them herself. She also feels motivated to increase her exercise levels by spending time regularly with her young granddaughter, taking her for increasingly energetic walks in the local park.

## Delegation

As she gains confidence in self-managing her diabetes, Shilpa needs less and less contact with her physician and nurse. She is a good candidate for the delegation approach because she can now largely manage her diabetes herself.

Shilpa has become an expert in understanding her own condition. She can see for herself how exercise, prudent eating, some modest weight loss and regular monitoring affect her glucose levels and this encourages her to maintain the lifestyle changes she has put in place. She never does attend the diabetes course, but she continues to have the follow-up blood tests which show that she is maintaining improvement. She feels encouraged and motivated to continue. She has also enlisted the support of family and friends and feels much more in control of her health.

## Supporting behaviour change during unplanned clinical consultations

Many patients struggle on with long-term conditions. They may have half-remembered information that was offered them when they were first diagnosed – and that may have been some time ago. They may be fearful of discovering that their condition has worsened. They may believe that asking for help is 'selfish' and that they should put up with their condition unless there is some emergency. They may ask for repeat prescriptions, but put off coming in for a review of their medication.

Yet sometimes this very patient may surprise you by suddenly requesting a consultation. For these unplanned and spontaneous consultations, it is worth exploring the reasons why a patient has chosen this particular time. For example, a celebrity whom they admire may have disclosed an illness with accompanying frankness about their treatment. A family member may have been taken ill. There may have been media stories about new treatments. Their motivation to address their health issues may be heightened as a result and can provide you with opportunities to encourage and support behaviour change through tailoring the way you discuss and present information:

> Jane has had asthma since childhood. She is 25 and a smoker. She has inhalers, but uses them sporadically and possibly ineffectively. Now she is notably more short of breath, may have a chest infection and is exhausted.

> Most of Jane's previous clinical encounters have been with practitioners who have focused on those enticing frequency–quantity closed questions: *how much? how many? how often?* In Jane's case these have been about whether or not she is using her inhalers and how much she smokes, followed by other closed questions in which practitioners have put themselves in the policing role: 'Have you thought about giving up smoking?' These practitioners experience Jane as hard work, they do most of the talking, following one closed question swiftly with another. They are frustrated by their inability to make any dent in her apparently self-destructive behaviour. For her part, Jane finds her clinicians high-handed and intrusive. She avoids contact with them wherever she can. She feels they see her as a case, not as an individual, and she protects her self-esteem by half-heartedly agreeing with

them, saying as little as possible or cleverly fobbing them off with half-truths.

Today's clinician, Owen, is different. He is welcoming, he is curious, saying it is good to see her, and he is intrigued to know what brings her to the consultation.

Jane says that her much-loved grandmother is in hospital with pneumonia and not doing well. 'She's only 58. She's always had asthma too, it runs in the family.'

Owen expresses concern, but resists the temptation to ask investigative questions about the grandmother because the focus here is on Jane. He asks a goal-setting question: 'So what should we be concentrating on today?'

Jane's reply tumbles out. She is scared, dreads the possibility of her grandmother's death, but also she is confused by her inhalers and worried about taking the preventer inhaler because she has read that they contain steroids and that maybe in the longer term it is not good to rely on them, as her grandmother has. She feels tired, she has difficulty climbing stairs without pausing for breath, now she also has frequent bouts of paroxysmal coughing. When she gets an attack, her boyfriend panics. 'I know I should give up the fags, but my boyfriend is a smoker too and I feel it would be hard to be a non-smoker around him because it would seem like I was being goody-goody.'

Owen realizes there is possibly too much to deal with in a single consultation. He hears the wheezy rattle in her chest as she coughs. He recognizes and manages his own anxiety about the risks this patient is running and his urge to concentrate on the inhaler problem. He summarizes by naming both issues, following this with 'I need to listen to your chest, so let's get that out of the way first'.

An examination quickly suggests that Jane has a chest infection and there is a brief conversation about the prescription.

Now, he returns to the rest of Jane's agenda, asking another goal-setting question, 'Which is the priority for you today – the inhalers or giving up the fags?'

Jane's immediate concern is with the inhalers.

'OK, so let's start with how much you already know about how inhalers work.'

The answer was 'very little'. So would it help to explain? Yes, it would. Despite having few artistic skills, Owen draws a diagram to show what happens to the lungs in asthma and also what the effect of smoking is on the lung airways. He then explains the way that the different inhalers work to reverse these effects and explained that stopping smoking would contribute substantially to this. He makes suggestions about how Jane should brief her boyfriend about what to do when she has an asthma attack. Then he says: 'But I've been doing a lot of talking. How does this strike you?'

'This is the first time anyone's bothered to explain any of it to me and it all makes sense.'

Then the discussion turns to the preventer inhaler where Jane's question was about how essential it was to take it every day, the long-term effects of steroids and whether it was possible to get an equally positive effect with a lower dose.

Finally, Owen returns to the subject of giving up smoking, aware of the danger of appearing not to have listened to Jane's hesitations. 'It really can be hard to do when you live with a fellow smoker and I understand your feelings about not wanting to seem goody-goody, but I'd like to help you further with that. How ready would you say you are to look at ways of stopping?'

'Maybe not quite yet, but you've made me think.'

'That's fine, you have to be ready, it's entirely up to you and motivation is everything. Just so that you know, we run a really good *Be a Non-Smoker* group here – it's free, it's fun and we get fantastic results. Here are the dates and times – you'd be very welcome. Just call to book your place.'

Jane leaves, clutching her not-very-well-drawn diagram, smiling and vowing to put it on her fridge.

In this consultation the clinician has conveyed concern and interest. It is possible that Jane's previous clinicians were also concerned and interested, but their poor communication skills got in the way. By staying non-judgemental, including resisting the temptation to use the chest infection as yet another way of frightening her, and by letting her set the agenda, he has uncovered her real anxieties, got beneath her brittle defences, enabled her to tell her story and to ask for the help she needs. Thanks to this, the chances are that this patient will use her medication properly and that, given time, she will also stop smoking.

## Multimorbidity and health coaching

Medication can be hazardous when managing patients with multimorbidity. Interactions between medications may produce adverse effects, and risks may rise further when the medication increases the likelihood of confusion and falls. Most national clinical guidelines focus on medication for single diseases and may not be immediately applicable to those patients with multimorbidity. The current pharmacological evidence base for treating multimorbidity is sparse, and when you are the prescriber you may need to use your clinical judgement based on experience, making compromises along the way. Drug administration can also present a burdensome anxiety for patients and their carers, as they try to make sense of the complex medication regimes they are being asked to follow. Many patients will not take their medications as prescribed, either by choice or because of their limited understanding of the reason for the prescriptions.[10]

Taking a health coaching approach for these patients can be a powerful way of identifying their priorities, using this as a basis for creating an individualized approach.

In the following case, some concentrated listening by the practitioner was the key to the kind of joint decision-making which would encourage and benefit the patient:

> Sidney is a 79-year-old with long-standing osteoarthritis and hypertension. He has also had a recent set of blood tests which indicate pre-diabetes. He currently takes a range of medications for his osteoarthritis-related pain, including paracetamol and co-codamol. The co-codamol makes him feel dizzy and drowsy. His primary care physician, Monica, has also prescribed two medications for his high blood pressure.

Sidney has not admitted to Monica that he takes the medications for his high blood pressure sporadically, for example when he has a headache, as he does not see it as a problem. He would much rather focus on being pain-free.

At his next appointment, his blood pressure remains high and Monica decides to take a different approach. She asks him about whether he has any worries about his medication, acknowledging that he has been given a number of different pills to take.

'I'm happy to take the painkillers as I know they make a difference but they sometimes make me feel dizzy. I live on my own and I'm afraid of having a fall.'

Listening quietly, Monica asks some prompting questions such as 'It sounds as if you might have some other questions about your pills …'.

Yes, he does. He is worried that taking the blood pressure tablets will cause him to feel more dizzy by giving him low blood pressure.

Together, Sidney and Monica agree a plan to stop the medication for high blood pressure and to adjust the type and dose of his pain medication to see if this helps the dizziness. They also discuss ways that he could have more support at home through involving his family and neighbours. Monica arranges to see him again after a few weeks to monitor his blood pressure and dizziness.

Over the next few months Sidney starts to feel more confident and the dizziness has settled. His blood pressure has remained high so he agrees to start taking one blood pressure tablet regularly as a trial. He feels more motivated to do this as he feels his doctor has understood and addressed his problems and he trusts her. He also feels more in control of his health as he has been involved in making the decisions about his medication.

## Coaching young patients

It is easy to assume that children and young people cannot be coached: they are too young, too immature, so they need to be *told*. In practice the same rules of human behaviour apply, whatever the patient's age. Lose rapport, do too much talking, press too hard, seem to be reproaching or patronizing and you will create resistance – and sometimes a disastrous loss of confidence, as in this example:

> When my 14-year-old son Sam was diagnosed with Type 1 diabetes, I was initially impressed with the approach the staff took with him. He was taught how to monitor his own blood sugar levels and how to inject himself with insulin. Sam was very positive about taking responsibility for himself. This proved tricky when it became apparent that giving the right amount of insulin to get a 'good' blood sugar reading was more complicated than he had thought, and I could see that he was losing patience and confidence. The first check-up visit to the hospital only reinforced his developing negative feelings, as health professionals pointed out, kindly enough, how far short Sam was failing against the blood sugar levels he 'should' be achieving and loaded him with advice and leaflets. His body language said it all – a mixture of teenage defiance and vulnerability.
>
> A year after initial diagnosis Sam was readmitted as an emergency with ketoacidosis. The clinical care was impressive, and he was soon feeling more comfortable. Much to my surprise, throughout his three-day stay, his blood sugar levels were read by nurses, who also administered his insulin. I did not see the nurses share the readings or discuss the insulin dose with him. In the hospital, it seemed that the experts took over and made everything 'right' again. The impression was that Sam had 'failed' and the professionals needed to be in charge. In preparation for going home, a specialist nurse came to see him and explained where he had been going wrong and gave out yet more leaflets. He said he found it condescending. He looked defensive and unhappy.
>
> No one, then or in the subsequent years, has talked to him about what was going well, what he thought the issues were, what might be helpful for him. No one has treated him as an equal. Conversations always seemed at best to be patronizing and with frequent notes of exasperation. He has learned to see himself as a *bad diabetic* – not a good place for developing the lifetime confidence

and resilience for managing such a complicated and difficult disease.

Compare this with the skilled treatment that Joshi has received. Joshi is aged 2. He still has only a limited vocabulary, though a sharp understanding of what people are saying to him. He has a genetically caused eye condition and is extremely short-sighted. Here, his dad describes how an ophthalmic paediatrician somehow managed to coach parents and toddler simultaneously:

Joshi is a happy, active and very wilful little boy! He would not wear his baby glasses – snatched them off as soon as we tried to put them on – what was this strange object being latched to his face? His favourite word is no! Trouble was he was running into things and getting more than the usual share of toddler mishaps because he saw obstructions too late. The consultant was really helpful at his last check-up. First she addressed all of us, not just my wife and me, did a lot of eye contact and had Joshi sitting close to her at her height on a specially boosted chair and she spent a lot of time just listening and asking some brief questions.

Then she leant towards Joshi with a big smile and asked him to take off her own glasses, which he did, and then to put them back on. I was then asked to count to ten slowly 'to see if the doctor can keep them on'. She watched him all the time, making funny faces. Then she held his glasses out to him, smiling broadly – 'Can you do the same, putting your glasses on and keeping them on, if Daddy counts to ten?' To my amazement he nodded. And did it!

'And now can you take them off?' Yes, he could. 'And put them back on again?'

And so it went on. He was in control the whole time. By the end of that session she had begun the process of showing him how much better he could see with glasses than without. With us, she gave us a running commentary on what she was doing and why, then we had a kind of brainstorming session about how we might adapt it and do the same at home. We never felt told off or discouraged, went away brimming with confidence and with Joshi grinning – with his glasses still on!

## How the health system can help

Increasingly, healthcare professionals are realizing that the system itself can support patient-centred care in a structured, planned way. There is also a move to commission specific health coaching services for selected groups of patients, and in particular those with long-term conditions.

An excellent example of implementing this type of service practice is the Diabetes *Year of Care* approach.[11] The Diabetes Year of Care, launched jointly by the charity Diabetes UK and the Department of Health in 2007, was an ambitious approach initially piloted in three diverse communities in the UK and now being adopted in other areas. The focus is on personalized care planning through collaborative conversations between healthcare professionals and patients. In this approach, patients with diabetes are proactively managed by sending them their blood results in advance, along with explanations of what this means for them. They are then better informed when they attend for their follow-up appointment with a nurse or doctor a few weeks later, where they are supported to consider what their results mean for them individually and to set goals that fit with their needs and priorities. It is easy to see how a coaching approach to healthcare conversations would fit well in this scenario, seamlessly enhancing existing approaches to empower patients with long-term conditions. Evaluation of the pilots demonstrated improved clinical outcomes, including blood pressure and diabetes control, improved diabetes care processes and data collection, improved experience of care and changes in self-care behaviour reported by patients with diabetes. Clinicians reported greater job satisfaction, better organization and team work. The House of Care metaphor[6] is an approach which developed from the Diabetes Year of Care, and highlights the need for a whole-systems approach with interdependent, key components: care planning, the engaged and informed patient, the healthcare professional committed to partnership working, organizational systems and processes, the local commissioning plan.

The House of Care metaphor[6] has highlighted the need for more flexibility in the length of appointments if this approach is to be embedded into routine practice. For instance, one of our medical colleagues wryly observed that with a standard 10-minute appointment, which in practice is a 7–8-minute appointment when taking into account the time it takes for a patient to enter the room and for writing up the consultation, there is just about enough time for the doctor to utter the magic words 'Be healed!' before it is time for the patient to leave.

## Commissioning health coaching for patients with long-term conditions

Organizations may commission health coaching around a set number of sessions, usually six or eight over several months, and coaching may be centred around a workbook tailored to a particular long-term condition. A trained health coach takes the patient through the book as in these projects:

> Birmingham Own Health was a telephone health coaching service set up in 2006 using nurses from NHS Direct to support patients with diabetes, chronic obstructive pulmonary disease or cardiac problems through monthly phone calls, working together through a series of eight modules where patients were supported to understand their conditions better and to make appropriate lifestyle changes. Evaluations[12] showed high patient satisfaction levels and improvements in clinical metrics (HbA1C levels and body mass index for patients with poorly controlled diabetes).

> In a bid to support local care pathways and promote better self-management of long-term conditions, clinical health coaching services run by Totally Health for patients with chronic obstructive pulmonary disease have been commissioned by a wide range of UK NHS organizations. The health coaches used are registered nurses who help patients to manage their condition through providing telephone-based mentoring and support.

In approaches such as these, patients may be identified for inclusion through risk stratification approaches which may target those at high risk, or those who may have frequent attendances as a result of their conditions. The health coach ensures that relevant information has been imparted to and understood by the patient, and the patient is invited to consider how this fits with their particular situation. The coach then helps the patient to set their own personal goals for what they want to achieve to better manage their health condition. This often involves approaches derived from motivational interviewing, identifying and addressing potential barriers, and identifying and putting in place factors that will increase the chances of success.

These approaches have many obvious attractions for the organizations which commission them. Workbooks give structure and may offer a degree of quality control. The approach is easy to replicate and therefore to roll out on a larger scale. Health coaches may only require a brief training period as they are largely guided by the format of the workbook. The standardized approach also lends itself to more effective evaluation processes.

There are limitations to be aware of. Relying exclusively on a workbook means that the agenda for the coaching sessions has already been set by the coach, so there is a danger that the coach may miss what really matters to the patient. Another issue is that these projects may be funded by the pharmaceutical industry, leading to questions about possibly competing agendas.

Advances in technology (see also page 7) have resulted in promising developments to combine health coaching approaches with mobile telehealth applications, providing powerful opportunities to personalize patient care.[13] Patients can monitor themselves in their own homes, for instance through home blood pressure readings or peak flow readings for asthma. They then send the data electronically to healthcare professionals. In remote areas, Skype calls are sometimes replacing face-to-face appointments. Increasingly, patients will also expect to communicate with practitioners using the methods that work best for them, for instance phone, FaceTime, text messages or emailed questions and prompts about appointments.

## Summary

Long-term conditions and how to manage them present one of the biggest single challenges in healthcare throughout the world when we are all living so much longer and when treatment can prolong life in ways that were previously impossible. Patients who present with multimorbidities may be especially challenging because drug interactions or drug-caused side effects may increase the complexities involved in making the best decisions. Health coaching can play a vital role in supporting and empowering patients with long-term conditions to manage their own health, for instance by exploring whole-life issues, listening intently, letting the patient set the agenda and taking every opportunity for a coaching conversation. A 'situational' approach may be valuable where the practitioner flexes their intervention according to what they judge the patient needs. There is also a range of ways in which coaching approaches can be integrated into existing services, for instance by commissioning specific health coaching services for selected groups of patients with long-term conditions.

# References

1. DeVol, R. and Bedroussian, A., with Charuworn, A., Chatterjee, A., Kim, I.K., Kim, S. and Klowden, K. *An Unhealthy America: The Economic Burden of Chronic Disease*. Santa Monica, CA: Milken Institute; 2007. http://www.milkeninstitute.org/publications/view/321 (accessed 10 February 2015).
2. Barnett, K., Mercer, S.W., Norbury, M., Watt, G., Wyke, S. and Guthrie, B. Epidemiology of multimorbidity and implications for health care, research, and medical education: a cross-sectional study. *Lancet* 2012; 380(9836): 37–43.
3. Hibbard, J. and Gilburt, H. *Supporting People to Manage Their Health: An Introduction to Patient Activation*. London: King's Fund; 2014. http://www.kingsfund.org.uk/sites/files/kf/field/field_publication_file/supporting-people-manage-health-patient-activation-may14.pdf (accessed 3 February 2015),
4. Epping-Jordan, J.E., Pruitt, S.D., Bengoa, R. and Wagner, E.H. Improving the quality of health care for chronic conditions. *Quality and Safety in Health Care* 2004; 13: 299–305.
5. Greene. J. and Hibbard, J.H. Why does patient activation matter? An examination of the relationships between patient activation and health-related outcomes. *Journal of General Internal Medicine* 2012; 27(5): 520–526.
6. Coulter, A., Roberts, S. and Dixon, A. *Delivering Better Services for People with Long-Term Conditions: Building the House of Care*. London: King's Fund; 2013. http://www.kingsfund.org.uk/sites/files/kf/field/field_publication_file/delivering-better-services-for-people-with-long-term-conditions.pdf (accessed 3 February 2015).
7. Royal College of General Practitioners. *An Inquiry into Patient Centred Care in the 21st Century*. London: RCGP; 2014. http://www.rcgp.org.uk/policy/rcgp-policy-areas/~/media/Files/Policy/A-Z-policy/RCGP-Inquiry-into-Patient-Centred-Care-in-the-21st-Century.ashx. (accessed 1 February 2015).
8. Driver, M. *Coaching Positively, Lesson for Coaches from Positive Psychology*. Maidenhead: Open University Press; 2011.
9. Hersey, P. and Blanchard, K.H. *Management of Organizational Behavior: Utilizing Human Resources* (3rd edition). Englewood Cliffs, NJ: Prentice Hall; 1977.
10. Marengoni, A. and Onder, G. Guidelines, polypharmacy, and drug-drug interactions in patients with multimorbidity. *British Medical Journal* 2015; 350: h1059.
11. Year of Care Partnerships. *Diabetes Year of Care Evaluation Report June 2011*. http://www.yearofcare.co.uk/sites/default/files/images/YOC_Report%20-%20correct.pdf (accessed 14 February 2015).

12. Jordan, R.E., Lancashire, R.J. and Adab, P. An evaluation of Birmingham Own Health telephone care management service among patients with poorly controlled diabetes. A retrospective comparison with the General Practice Research Database. *BMC Public Health* 2011; 11: 707.
13. Garland J. *Combine health coaching and telehealth to manage LTCs*; 2013. http://www.primarycaretoday.co.uk/nursing/combine-health-coaching-and-telehealth-manage-ltcs (accessed 3 February 2015).

# 7 EMPOWERING THE DISEMPOWERED PATIENT

One of the hesitations about applying coaching principles to health-care is the one where clinicians say, 'So many patients just want you to tell them what to do. How do you get around that?'

> As a physio I work with a lot of young athletes whose parents and coaches seem to have 100 per cent controlled their lives. There is a kind of helplessness about them when you ask them to decide something for themselves.

> Mr P is not at all well off and grew up at a time when doctors were gods. He enters the room very carefully as if on tiptoe, is tremendously respectful, nods constantly and never asks questions. The temptation just to deliver a mini-homily or quickly write the prescription at each consultation is overwhelming.

> He had just come out of prison and it struck me that he was amazed to be addressed as Mr [name].

> This patient has had a long series of setbacks, both medical and in her personal life. If I ask her a question there is a long silence and she looks away and says, 'I don't really know' and if I offer her choices, she says, 'Well you're the doctor, you know best I'm sure'.

One of the principles of health coaching is that the clinician and patient are equals, but how can this work when a significant number of the patient population appears to be so disempowered: too overawed, too passive, too timid, seemingly unable or unwilling to take responsibility for their own health? Our aim in this chapter is to explore why this happens and how, despite all of this, you can still work in coaching style with such patients.

## What is disempowerment?

One way of looking at disempowerment is to see it as a low level of what psychologists call *sense of agency*, also known as *self-efficacy*. This is closely related to another useful psychological concept, *locus of control*, first described by the American psychologist Julian B. Rotter.[1] You could have an internal or an external locus of control, and there are profound psychological consequences to being at either end of the spectrum.

With an *external* locus of control you believe that luck determines much of what happens to you. If you are in the right place at the right time then things will work out well. If they do not, then it is because you were unlucky – you did not know the right people and others did. When you face risk, you may shrug your shoulders because fate decides outcomes on a whim and you do not believe it will make much difference to take precautions to protect yourself. You feel powerless when it comes to affecting whether people like you or not. When things go wrong you will be more likely to blame others or external events. Depression and stress may sometimes result from your feelings of anger and helplessness.

With an *internal* locus of control you believe you are in charge of your own life, you can act to change people and events. Where there is risk, for instance to your health, you will take sensible precautions because you believe that this will pay off. If you experience a disappointment, you will take at least some responsibility for what happened and be determined to learn from it so that you minimize the chances of a repeat. You believe that effort will pay off and that luck has nothing much to do with what happens to you. You are confident that good interpersonal skills will go a long way towards making life enjoyable. You rarely experience depression, and feel that stress is something that can be managed.

A disempowered patient is highly likely to have an external locus of control, that is, in health terms they may not value their own well-being, may feel that nothing they do will affect the outcomes and that authority figures such as clinicians should make decisions for them.

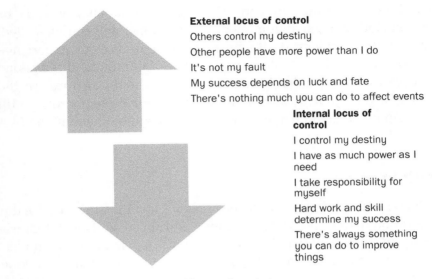

**External locus of control**

Others control my destiny

Other people have more power than I do

It's not my fault

My success depends on luck and fate

There's nothing much you can do to affect events

**Internal locus of control**

I control my destiny

I have as much power as I need

I take responsibility for myself

Hard work and skill determine my success

There's always something you can do to improve things

**Figure 7.1** External versus internal locus of control

# The origins of disempowerment

There is no one factor that creates disempowerment and in practice it is likely to be a blend of inborn temperament, the impact of parenting style, cultural pressures and life experience. The more of these that have combined to rob people of their natural needs for autonomy and competence (see also Chapter 2), especially when they have experienced repeated setbacks, the more likely it is that learned helplessness will be the result. They may have a low internal level of resilience, for example, in the face of challenging life experiences, dysfunctional family dynamics or socioeconomic difficulties. Redundancy or the threat of redundancy in an uncertain economic climate can have a major impact on a patient's stress levels, leaving them with feelings of failure and rejection. Factors such as language barriers, cultural and gender differences, age, disabilities, perceived social status and level of education may all play their part.

The healthcare system itself may also contribute to the problem. Appointments may be inconveniently timed for patients in jobs or organizations which are unforgiving about absence. It may be impossible for them to take time off without losing money; there may be difficulties in arranging childcare. Then when the patient arrives he or she might find that the appointment has inexplicably been cancelled. Getting an appointment at all may have been an anxious experience when you have to book online or negotiate an automated telephone system which may randomly hang up on you mid-way through the call, or you find yourself unable to explain your problem coherently and briefly to a receptionist in order to get the appointment in the first place.

## Health literacy

Health literacy is an important determinant of health. The World Health Organization defines it as 'The cognitive and social skills which determine the motivation and ability of individuals to gain access to, understand and use information in ways which promote and maintain good health'.[2]

Research[3] suggests that low levels of health literacy are associated with a higher prevalence of conditions such as diabetes and heart failure, and with poorer reported levels of physical and mental health. When your levels of health literacy are low, you are more likely to access emergency services or to be admitted to hospital, and less likely to engage with preventative health activities such as screening. Low levels of health literacy are most common in patients from disadvantaged populations and with low basic skills. The research[4] here is shocking in what it reveals. It tells us that 43 per cent of the adult working population in England is unable to fully understand or use health information based on text. This proportion rises to 61 per cent when numerical information is included. Low levels of health literacy are more common among older people, black and ethnic minority groups and those with rudimentary levels of qualifications.[5]

Genuinely shared decision-making by patients can only happen if they have an adequate level of health literacy. Well-meant efforts to share decision-making can be wrecked if the patient simply does not have the information to understand what is at stake:

> Dorothy is a 75-year-old Londoner who has been diagnosed with breast cancer. She worked in poorly paid jobs until she retired ten years ago. She tells her friends and family about her outrage at the behaviour of her young oncologist. 'He told me I needed

to decide whether I wanted surgery now or to give some pills a chance to reduce the tumour first. Why did he ask that? It was ridiculous! He used long words to talk about side effects, recovery, percentage this, percentage that. How could I know?'

This is why increasing the health literacy of patients is so important, as it is a precursor to feeling empowered enough to take control of their own health. (See Chapter 5 for suggestions about how to communicate information in a way that patients are likely to understand and use.)

## Judging your patient

As healthcare professionals, we can also unwittingly contribute to people's feelings of disempowerment. For instance, the patient may have to negotiate a closed door to the consultation room – is he or she expected to knock or not? There may be a polished leather chair for the clinician. This chair may be set at a higher level than the shabbier one intended for the patient. We may fail to greet the patient, paying more attention to the computer screen or to finishing a telephone call. There may be more subtle social cues which create imbalances of power, so a half-finished cup of coffee on your desk may suggest that the patient is interrupting you.

As clinicians we may pride ourselves on being unprejudiced and open, but we are only human and it is inevitable that we hold private opinions and judgements about certain groups, such as those of a different sex or cultural background, those who speak a different language, the disabled, the homeless, the refugees, the asylum seekers, offenders, travellers, the obese – the list is endless and may influence the tone and direction of the consultation.

Despite your best efforts at keeping the relationship on an equal footing, the relationship is bound to be affected by subtle or overt differences between you and the patient. Much of this may work at a subconscious level, but can significantly affect the outcomes:

I am a primary care physician and I have done a considerable amount of training in health coaching. I was seeing a 2-year-old girl for asthma monitoring. The child's mother, was an 18-year-old, Lisa, who was not in a relationship, and was living with her own mother.

Lisa and her mother are both heavy smokers. I immediately noticed the strong smell of cigarette smoke as Lisa came in. I simply couldn't help thinking, 'Lisa is smoking in front of this little daughter and this is so wrong!' I believed that this was irresponsible behaviour and that it was making her daughter's illness worse. I was aware of making this judgement and also that I knew I should not be. Nevertheless, I thought I should try using a coaching approach. Unfortunately I was thinking of this as I was trying to get Lisa to see the error of her ways so my way of doing this was to offer her advice in disguise.

'I'm sure you know that your own heavy smoking is making your child's asthma worse. Do you think it would be a good idea to stop?'

I followed this by asking a good coaching question but I delivered it in an irritated tone: 'What's stopping you giving up?'

Needless to say, this approach got precisely nowhere. I got a mumbled reply. Result: a total lose–lose. I felt annoyed and disappointed and Lisa felt reproached and was no nearer to giving up smoking.

So even when you train in coaching skills and at some level know perfectly well that you are being judgemental, it can be very hard to stop when your own deeply held values are challenged by a patient who does not appear to share them.

It is impossible to coach someone effectively when you are coming from a position of judgement. When working with patients who may be feeling disempowered, the first step is to pay attention to your own mindset – what are your feelings towards this patient? Are you able to work with them non-judgementally? Are you able to respect them? Do you believe they are resourceful? These conditions are prerequisites for a coaching conversation. If they are not present for whatever reason, and if you are unable to move to a different frame of mind, then a coaching conversation will not be the right intervention for you to use at this time (see also Chapter 2).

# The danger of rescuing

Healthcare professionals want to make a difference. Because of this, we often try to take on a helper and problem-solver role, believing that this is what the patient most needs. This may be important and necessary in some circumstances, but is also accompanied by the risk of further disempowering the patient, and, in transactional analysis terms, inadvertently setting up a parent–child or victim–rescuer–persecutor dynamic (see page 54). When working with a patient who seems disempowered, it is important to bring this into conscious awareness. If you do not, the consequences can be dire:

James has been a primary care physician for over 20 years. He experienced a period of disillusionment about his medical career, questioning his role and purpose. But his enthusiasm was reignited after attending a course on consultation skills. He rapidly became a skilled rapport-builder and developed a loyal following of vulnerable patients who felt genuinely helped and listened to by a doctor who seemed to care so much about them. James found these relationships fulfilling.

Gradually, James began to feel overwhelmed by the level of dependency some of his patients were exhibiting. In particular, there was Mrs R, who had experienced a difficult childhood and had pressing issues of self-esteem and confidence. She was unemployed and had severe financial problems. These contributed to instability over housing and intermittent periods of homelessness. After her relationship broke up she started drinking heavily. James had supported her generously with his time during this period.

She started to book more frequent consultations, and despite her straitened financial situation, began to bring him little gifts. James became increasingly alarmed by this unwanted attention and after discussion with a colleague, he spoke to Mrs R explaining that he could not accept the gifts and suggested, as tactfully as he could, that it would be better for her to see another doctor.

Mrs R was upset and angry, shouting at him and telling him that he was a disgracefully bad doctor. She subsequently made a formal complaint to the practice, claiming that James had never been interested in helping her and that he had been rude.

This case illustrates the dangers that can arise from well-meant but dysfunctional clinician–patient relationships. If you use the lens of the drama triangle (see page 54) to reflect on what may be happening here you will see that through James's strong desire to help his patients, particularly those who are more vulnerable, he has subconsciously set himself up in the unwinnable role of rescuer, keen to fix their problems because he gets such a strong sense of personal reward from it. Mrs R in turn has taken on a victim role, reinforced through her interactions with him. Initially both people see this as beneficial. However, it does not take long for roles to switch, with James briefly appearing to be the persecutor as he tells Mrs R to see a different doctor after rejecting her gifts. Mrs R then switches rapidly to a persecutor role with James now in a victim role, as she becomes abusive and makes a complaint against him.

This common situation can create enormous levels of anxiety and possibly medico-legal consequences for a practitioner who initially invested a huge amount of time and emotional energy in a strong desire to help a patient. Far from helping, attempts to rescue can inadvertently lead to further disempowerment for an already disempowered patient. It also demonstrates that disempowerment does not mean inability to act.

## Watching out for assumptions

Appearances can deceive. Some patients may seem easily recognizable as 'disempowered' because of the severity of their disability, their inability to speak English or their marginalized social status. But things may not be what they seem, as these clinicians' rueful accounts demonstrate:

> I'm part of the mobile TB prevention unit that takes our service direct to high-risk groups. We were visiting a charity which provides free lunches to homeless people and there was a short queue of men waiting to get into the trailer. I thought one of them looked a little restless and his appearance was also quite odd as, although he looked dishevelled and a bit grubby, he was dressed in full transvestite rig. I touched him lightly on the arm and said, 'Won't be long now'. He whipped round glaring at me and said, 'Don't you know it's rude to touch?'

> My patient came to the consultation with an interpreter. He was an elderly man, thin and stooped and was an asylum seeker from a French-speaking African country. He described symptoms which could mean prostate problems. I began to explain in what I now

realize was highly simplistic language what the prostate was. He rolled his eyes, looked at his interpreter and spoke a few words in French which I did sort of understand. These were to the effect that did this dim person – me – think he was an idiot? Of course he knew what the prostate was. The interpreter spotted that I had understood this and said something in rapid French to which the patient replied. The interpreter explained that my patient had been a distinguished university professor in his country. I felt it was only right that I gathered together enough halting French to talk to him direct. This earned me a smile, which I think I probably did not deserve.

## The resourceful, resilient patient

It pays to assume that the patient is resourceful – often far more resourceful than we think. Our role as practitioners then shifts from expert to facilitator, genuinely empowering the patient to tap into their own courage and energy, increasing their levels of resilience as they navigate through their challenges.

It is perfectly possible that you as the healthcare professional may be the first and only person to whom the patient feels able to talk about their issues. These can often be complex and feel overwhelming and unmanageable for both them and you. The patient is far more likely to believe in their own resourcefulness if they sense that you believe this too. A coaching approach can be a powerful way to empower a disempowered patient. When you do this you help them to clarify their thinking through using skills such as active listening, summarizing, reflecting and offering feedback, helping them to set realistic, achievable goals, and asking them questions that enable them to use their own resourcefulness to identify a way forward that would work best for them (see also Chapter 3).

Questions that are particularly useful with disempowered patients include:

What's going right?

What part of this do you have control over?

In an ideal world, what do you want?

What sources of support do you have?

How motivated are you to achieve your goal?

What would need to happen for that motivation to increase?

What's your next step?

## Increasing the patient's sense of resourcefulness

A patient who appears to be disempowered can be challenging. You make suggestions, but the patient doesn't act on them; you prescribe medication and the patient does not complete the course; you make follow-up appointments but the patient does not attend; you listen carefully but somehow there is a sense that you are not truly connecting.

Sometimes, the answer is to concentrate not so much on the presenting issue as on how to increase the patient's sense that they do have at least some control over their own lives:

> Jackie is 42. She has been in a violent and abusive relationship with her husband for 8 years. She left her husband a year ago and since then has been seeing her doctor, Antonia, for symptoms of depression.
>
> Jackie repeats her story to Antonia. 'I feel so isolated, my Mum lives a long way away and anyway she's a bit frail, I can't stand my husband's family and a lot of my friends have moved away.' She adds that her part-time admin job is the only thing that motivates her to leave the house.
>
> In previous conversations, Antonia has discussed counselling, but Jackie has refused to consider it. 'I don't think it would help. How would just talking to someone do me any good?'
>
> 'How are you getting on with the pills?' asks Antonia.
>
> Jackie looks away. 'I forget to take them sometimes.'
>
> Antonia realizes that these consultations have fallen into an ineffectual pattern, which has been that she asks how the antidepressant medication is going and then makes adjustments to the dose without anything significantly changing for the patient. Antonia has recently been on a coaching course and, reflecting

on the lack of progress she is making, decides to give the coaching approach a try, since nothing else seems to be working. She starts by asking a powerful coaching question:

'What advice would you give yourself if you were feeling at your most confident and resourceful?'

There is a long pause. 'I haven't felt confident for years, so I don't know – it all went wrong after I got married.'

'So tell me what you were like before that.'

'I was a confident, happy person. I loved arts and crafts, sewing, knitting...'

As she said this, Jackie became more animated and for the first time made proper eye contact. Noticing this change, Antonia remarked on it, following this with 'So what advice would this earlier version of yourself give to the person sitting here now?'

Jackie smiled tentatively as she answered that it would probably be about restarting something creative like sewing. The next few minutes of the conversation were about how she would go about doing this. This proved to be a turning point and over the next few months, through putting energy into her creative interests, she started to regain her self-confidence. Her depression lifted as she began sewing gifts for friends and family, which led to a sense of purpose and also reduced her feelings of isolation.

## The role of social support in developing resilience

We know that adverse economic conditions can worsen health-related quality of life, and may also have a negative impact on mental health. For instance, poverty is a risk factor for suicide. Research tells us that social support reduces these effects because it serves as an independent protective factor for health.[6] When coaching patients whose health is being affected by the economic climate, it may be vital to work with them on identifying who in their social network might support them:

I now routinely ask patients about their support systems. I have a variety of useful questions here, such as 'Who can support you here?' or 'Who are you closest to?' and 'Who among your family, friends or neighbours can be of help?' Then I take it down a layer to find out more about what kind of help – quality, frequency and so on.

Often patients will be able to identify people in their network but are reluctant to ask them. I may now spend as much time in the consultation on this as I used to spend wittering away about their medication, in effect coaching them through how to ask family and friends for what they need.

If patients' own sources of support are limited, then it can help to direct them to whatever community resources are available, making sure that your own information is up to date. Offering this information, using the coaching approach described in Chapter 5, increases the likelihood that patients will absorb it, deciding for themselves whether they will follow it up.

## Coaching across cultural barriers

Working with diverse patient populations can be a rich and rewarding experience. It also presents challenges.

### Ideas about illness

There are startling differences between cultures in the ideas they hold about health. In many cultures, people do not share the Western medical understanding of the body as a complex organism where disease can be scientifically explained. People may believe that illness is a punishment for sin. For instance, there are cultures where illness is seen as retribution for failing to carry out the proper rituals for a dead ancestor, or for failing to appease a deity with the correct offerings. Or it might just be perceived as your fate:

> I was discussing diet, lifestyle and medication for her Type 2 diabetes with a patient who had recently arrived from Bangladesh to join her British husband. Fortunately, I did spot from minute hesitations in how she responded to me that there was some problem. I gently pressed her on this. Although her English was not wonderful, I did understand her explanation that diabetes was just 'bad karma' so it had nothing to do with lifestyle and there wasn't a lot of point in taking medication, though she told me she had been consulting a 'spiritual healer' who was also an Ayurvedic practitioner.

Working as a dentist in London in an area with a large African population, I've sometimes had conversations with the mums of little kids with extensive caries where the mum has told me with absolute certainty that the child's tooth problems are the work of evil spirits. I know now how to acknowledge this belief without even raising an eyebrow, and I talk about how modern dentistry is more than a match for evil spirits and that evil spirits adore the sugar which is what has actually caused the problem, so keeping sugar away from teeth will also keep the evil spirits away. Given how I feel about the sugar industry, this is not so far from the truth!

The concept of preventative medicine, asymptomatic disease and routine appointments may also be poorly understood in some cultures. Remission, for instance, may be seen as cure. Patients who share this belief may seek help when they feel ill but not otherwise:

Some of our patients don't keep follow-up appointments because they feel better, so what is the point? This happens also with immunizations. Their child screamed at the first batch, so why subject her to more when she's not actually ill? They accept the appointment card but politeness plus fear of openly contradicting authority prevents them from saying they don't think it's necessary.

Custom may dictate what can and cannot be talked about openly. So in some Asian communities it is taboo to speak about death to a patient with a terminal illness. The conversation may need to be mediated through a senior family member. Family systems may be different, so in some cultures, the views of other family members may need to be taken into account:

My patient was a Nigerian woman in a very senior and well-paid job finding it difficult to keep on top of work as well as being a mother and a wife. She was struggling with the stress which was making her hypertension a lot worse. Despite her high status in a British organization, she frequently raised objections to treatment suggestions or to non-medical ways to alleviate her stress by saying that her Ghanaian mother-in-law and her husband's brothers might object. Over the years I have learnt to accept the wise words of a colleague who said, 'never forget the influence of Grandma!'

There are many parts of the world where mental illness is considered to be the work of devils. There are others where learning disability and mental illness are considered shaming. This British doctor of Chinese descent describes how difficult it can be to coax patients into talking about their symptoms:

> My parents came from Hong Kong and I have visited grandparents in China many times, so I know how deeply you can fear losing face if you admit to any illness that is not physical in cause. There can also be a reluctance to disclose anything that is truly personal. My Chinese patients do trust me because I look like them and I can speak to them in Mandarin, but even so they will often go all round the houses talking about vague aches and pains before they will admit to what is actually depression or chronic anxiety. Medication has to be taken in secret and they will conceal the diagnosis from family and Chinese friends, making up some explanation like 'migraine' or 'stomach flu'.

## Differences in healthcare systems

Healthcare systems in the patient's country of origin may be differently organized, so if the home custom is to queue on a first-come-first-served basis, a patient who does not attend may believe they are merely freeing up the doctor's time for another patient, rather than upsetting an intricately balanced appointments system. There may be radical differences in the status of doctors and the typical relationship that people expect with a clinician. In Western societies a doctor's status is based on qualifications. But in some African societies, for instance, people will get referrals to a healer from a friend or family member and will expect overt warmth and rapport, with many questions about the well-being of the family before the consultation begins. They may experience the lack of this in a Western clinician with consternation and disappointment.

Doctors and other health professionals in some cultures and healthcare systems may actively discourage patients from questioning or discussing their condition and treatment. A patient who is used to this may view our own attempts at collaboration with dismay and suspicion – or just bafflement:

> Mrs Y has settled in the UK from an eastern European country where I know that some doctors behave in a highly authoritarian

way. She speaks reasonable English. My attempts to smile at her, to encourage her to talk and ask questions are all met with sweet smiles and nods – and no questions. She says, 'Yes, OK, OK' repeatedly, but I have no idea what's going on for her.

I have some Spanish patients who tell me that in some country areas it is still perfectly normal for the patient to stand up throughout the entire consultation, usually very brief, while the doctor sits down. They tell me it feels 'weird' to be treated as an equal and I can see that they don't truly understand it.

## Interpreters

When a patient does not speak the same language as you, some form of interpretation may be necessary. It is good practice to use an independent interpreter rather than a family member, because this will safeguard patient confidentiality and increase the chances of an open, honest discussion. Arrange three identical chairs, for healthcare professional, patient and interpreter, equidistant from each other. You should speak directly to the patient rather than to the interpreter and encourage the patient to do the same. The interpreter should be appropriately trained, knowing how important it is to translate accurately without superimposing their own values or meanings. Using an interpreter will always take more time, so you will need to allow for this, for instance by booking a double-length appointment.

We believe that all of these factors are essential if a high-quality clinical consultation is to take place when using an interpreter. In practice, healthcare professionals often take shortcuts because they are under time pressure or have had little training in working in this way. When this happens the consultation is set up for failure.

But take heart, it is still possible to take a coaching approach, even when so many factors seem to preclude it:

> Sadia is 34 years old and is from Afghanistan. She speaks very little English. She has four children and moved to London with her husband and family last year. The family now has refugee status. She has been attending the surgery frequently with her children for a range of health issues, including asthma and eczema in her children and her own musculoskeletal pain symptoms, which started when she came to the UK.

Sadia describes her housing as cramped, dirty and damp. She has been seeing a counsellor and is under follow-up from the local musculoskeletal service. She does not usually have a professional interpreter for her consultation. Instead, her young children have translated for her. Her usual clinician, Carolyn, was often left feeling frustrated after the consultations as she could not find a way to help this patient and her family to move forward.

Carolyn decided to try a coaching approach. She invited Sadia back for a double appointment lasting 20 minutes and booked a professional interpreter. She explained to Sadia that she felt unsure about how best to help her but was going to ask her some different questions.

'If you could create your ideal world, what would be happening?'

Sadia responded quickly. 'I'd have a much better relationship with my husband.' She said he was very kind and loving but was working hard doing long shifts to earn more money for the family and that she saw very little of him.

'I feel so isolated and I've got to deal with all the family's problems on my own.' This response was accompanied by a significant shift in Sadia's body language, with an immediately more relaxed posture and slower breathing.

This opened up a new discussion about what she could do to improve her marital relationship. Then the discussion went on to how she might feel more supported and less isolated.

Carolyn was able to tell her about a local Afghan women's voluntary organization for community support, and Sadia also resolved to make time that evening to speak to her husband and tell him how she was feeling. Over the next few months, she reported a definite improvement in her marital relationship. She felt they were working more as a team, which enabled them both to take on the challenges of addressing their housing problems. She started to engage more effectively with her counsellor, as well as making new friends through the Afghan women's organization. Her musculoskeletal symptoms became less severe and she also felt more motivated to manage her children's asthma and eczema symptoms by using the medication as prescribed.

## Variations in non-verbal communication

When working with a patient from a different cultural background, or indeed someone of a different gender or age, it is important to be aware that the significance that they may attribute to some types of body language may be different from your own. For example, those with an American or European background may place a high value on eye contact as an indicator of engagement and level of interest. In contrast, those from other cultural backgrounds may see direct eye contact as a sign of rudeness and disrespect. The meaning of certain hand gestures can also vary greatly, and different attitudes may exist about the significance and value of touch in the consultation process. For example, a hand on the shoulder or shaking hands may be seen within some cultures as a step towards building rapport but may also have the opposite effect for someone from a culture where touch is seen as taboo, particularly between a man and a woman.

Be wary of interpreting emotions or levels of pain based on only on a patient's facial expression, as this can also vary greatly. In general, it is best to follow the patient's lead. For example, where touch and use of physical space is concerned, if the patient seems comfortable to move closer to you and to touch, then this may be a sign of what is acceptable to them. If they seem uncomfortable, and if you do not need to enter their physical space clinically, then avoid it. Similarly with eye contact, if a patient is not making eye contact in the way you would normally expect, be sensitive to the possibility that this may be because they interpret the meaning of eye contact differently, rather than because they are uninterested. If in doubt, just ask, for instance by offering an observation: 'I noticed that you looked away when we started speaking about...' and ask the patient about what this lack of eye contact meant for them.

## The impact of language styles

Communication styles can vary hugely between languages and cultures. For instance, people from an older generation, and from more traditional societies, may prefer to be addressed formally through the use of their surname, regardless of how well they feel they know you. Not to do so may be interpreted as a sign of disrespect. If in doubt, ask the patient how they would prefer to be addressed – this can sometimes make all the difference to developing rapport based on mutual respect and so to the outcome of the consultation:

> I winced every time I heard people in the care home address my father as 'Albert'. He had never used this first name so he constantly corrected them, saying, 'My name's Bill, it's Bill' but really, he told me, he'd rather have been addressed by his surname.

> My mother grew up in Bulgaria. She has never adjusted to British informality and tells me that she feels overcome with embarrassment every time her breezy young doctor encourages her to address him by his first name.

The English language can predispose to a more direct communication style, whereas some cultures may prefer to answer a question less directly, for example through using storytelling. Being aware of this can prevent misunderstandings. Listen carefully to the way the patient tells their story. Ask open-ended questions, encourage the patient to continue so that you get to the heart of the story.

## Metaphorical and 'clean' language

Patients may also use metaphors in different ways depending on their language, culture and gender. For instance, for many Indian languages, the terminology used to describe physical pain may be indistinguishable from that used to describe emotional suffering. This can be the source of much misunderstanding when communicating across cultures. Earlier in this book (see page 62) we described the concept of clean language. This involves becoming aware of and temporarily suspending our own assumptions about what the meaning of a person's communication may be. Instead you ask specific questions to drill down further:

> In this example, a 77-year-old Indian patient lives with her extended family and presents to a primary care physician with 'a pain in the heart':

Patient: I feel a burning pain in my heart area.

Doctor: Is the pain sharp or dull?

Patient: Just burning

Doctor: Does it feel like a pressing pain or like a needle?

Patient: Neither – it is just like my heart is on fire!

Doctor: Does the pain go anywhere?

Patient: My whole body feels hot.

Doctor: Is it worse when you exercise or when you eat?

Patient: It is there all the time, especially when I am at home, it never goes away and I feel like I am going to die!

Doctor: Has the pain been getting worse or better?

Patient: Worse over the last few weeks.

Following a normal physical examination, the doctor decides to refer the patient to the local chest pain clinic for further investigations to rule out a cardiac cause. The clinic discharges her following normal results.

She re-presents a month later to a different doctor with the same symptoms. The second doctor follows a 'clean language' approach. This results in a very different interaction:

Patient: I feel a burning pain in my heart area.

Doctor: Can you tell me more about what you feel?

Patient: It feels burning hot, like there is a fire in my heart and it spreads through my whole body.

Doctor: And what is that like for you?

Patient: I feel very scared ... [pause]

Doctor: Scared?

Patient: Yes ... and angry too, very angry.

Doctor: Angry?

Patient: Angry that my family don't seem to care about me, don't want to help me, and then my heart is set on fire.

Doctor: And what would it feel like for you if the fire was not there anymore?

Patient: I wouldn't feel like I was a burden to my family ... I would feel wanted and valued by them.

After asking a few more questions about the nature of the pain, and conducting yet another physical examination which was normal, the doctor went on to explore with the patient how she might go about expressing her feelings to her family and also about her emerging care needs. Over the next few weeks and months, with the coaching of her doctor, her relationship with the other members of her family improved as they came to a greater understanding of her fears and vulnerabilities. They supported her to obtain practical help through carers. The patient was then able to feel a greatly increased sense of independence as well as feeling valued by her family.

## Summary

In this chapter, we have explored some of the factors which may result in a patient feeling disempowered, including those relating to the patient's circumstances, the healthcare professional and the wider system. A non-judgemental mindset is an essential prerequisite for using a coaching approach with a patient as this makes it more likely that you will be able to make a relationship based on mutual respect and a belief in the patient's own resourcefulness. An internal locus of control and low levels of health literacy are common in disadvantaged groups, limiting their ability to take charge of their own health. Using a coaching approach can enhance a patient's health literacy, increasing the likelihood of genuine empowerment. Social support has an important role in developing resilience, and it can be essential to have accurate and up-to-date information about what is available in the community as well as in the patient's own family and friendship groups. Coaching a patient across language or cultural barriers may include working effectively with interpreters, staying aware of our own generalizations and prejudices and of variations in non-verbal communication and language styles. A coaching approach may be a powerful way of empowering a disempowered patient to develop their resilience and to use their own resourcefulness to identify and achieve their health-related goals.

## References

1. Rotter, J.B. Generalized expectancies for internal versus external control of reinforcement. *Psychological Monographs: General and Applied* 1966; 80(1): 1–28.
2. World Health Organization. *Health Promotion Glossary*. Geneva: WHO; 1998.

3. Berkman, N.D., Sheridan, S.L., Donahue, K.E. *et al. Health Literacy Interventions and Outcomes: An Updated Systematic Review.* Report no. 199. Rockville, MD: Agency for Healthcare Research and Quality; 2011.

4. Rowlands, G., Protheroe, J., Winkley, J., Richardson, M., Seed, P.T., Rudd, R. A mismatch between population health literacy and the complexity of health information: An observational study. *British Journal of General Practice* 2015; 65(635): e379–e386.

5. Greenhalgh, T. Health literacy: towards system level solutions. *British Medical Journal* 2015; 350: h1026.

6. Fernandez, A., Garcia Alonso, J., Royo-Pastor, C., Garell-Corbera, I., Rengel-Chica, J., Agudo-Uena, J., Ramos, A. and Mendive, J.M. Effects of the economic crisis and social support on health related quality of life. *British Journal General Practice* 2015; 65(632): 134–136.

# 8 MIND MATTERS: COACHING FOR RECOVERY IN MENTAL HEALTH

We believe in the validity of the coaching approach for any branch of healthcare, but how can it work in mental health? When, as the argument may go, so many of the users of mental health services are severely incapacitated by their illnesses, might this be the exception? Our answer is that we believe the coaching approach to be just as useful in mental health as it is in other types of healthcare, and in this chapter we describe how you might apply it.

## The recovery approach in mental health

The traditional approach to psychiatry is based on the concept of *clinical recovery*. This relates to the aim of helping the service user eliminate or reduce symptoms, enabling them to function effectively again on a social level. In contrast, the concept of *personal recovery* has been defined as a

> deeply personal and unique process of changing one's attitudes, values, feelings, goals, skills and/or roles. It is a way of living a satisfying, hopeful and contributing life, even within the limitations caused by illness. Recovery involves the development of new meaning and purpose in one's life as one grows beyond the catastrophic effects of mental illness.[1]

The values of this approach are closely aligned with those of the coaching process we have described in this book, and it is no surprise that practitioners who want to work in this way see coaching as the most promising style to adopt.

## Recovery principles

The recovery approach is characterized by three principles:

*Hope.* This assumes optimism about the future and that people can get well enough to keep their symptoms under control. There are parallels here with the person-centred approach to managing patients with long-term physical conditions, working with the notion that they are resilient and resourceful.

*Agency.* This assumes that patients can take control of their lives and that recovery is not something done *to* the person but something that they manage for themselves because they know their own condition, their own life and what they really want better than any clinician can. This means that it is the patient who defines their goals not the clinician. The clinician's role is to facilitate recovery, not to coerce or control.

*Opportunity.* This assumes that patients want to be connected to the wider groups they live in and that they can participate fully as citizens, as family members and as people who can contribute.

An influential paper, *Recovery Is for All: Hope, Agency and Opportunity in Psychiatry,*[2] says:

[Recovery] will mean a shift in the relationship between professionals and service users to one with a greater emphasis on partnership. It represents a transfer of authority to define and recognise [recovery] away from the professional to the individual.

## Differences between recovery and traditional approaches to mental health

There are profound differences between this approach and the traditional way of dealing with people who have mental health problems. We summarize them in Table 8.1.

Looking back to the early 2000s, one doctor, then a young trainee, writes of the difficulty she experienced in trying to implement the recovery approach:

I had at the time completed a coaching course and did have success with coaching conversations with some of my patients

**Table 8.1**   Traditional and recovery approaches to mental illness

| Traditional approach | Recovery approach |
| --- | --- |
| Mental illness has a biological basis; people have a genetic predisposition to such illnesses | Mental illness is a complex response to challenging social circumstances in which genes may play a part |
| Drugs are our most powerful allies in treating mental disorders | Drugs may be helpful for some people but listening empathetically to their story is often more important |
| Classifying and diagnosing is the foundation of treatment and is where clinicians add most value | Diagnosis is an imprecise art. Clinicians add most value by co-creating a relationship with service users and their families. Talking therapy with or without drugs often gives a better outcome than drugs alone |
| The goal of treatment is to reduce the worst of the symptoms | The goal of treatment is to work to the service user's goals and to assume that the overall quality of their lives is what will matter to them |
| Doctors need to lead treatment protocols | A team approach is healthier; the team can be led by anyone skilled in a whole suite of relevant clinical skills and knowledge |
| People who are mentally ill should agree to conform to what their psychiatrists think is best for them | Relationship is everything. The 'therapeutic alliance' is the foundation; without it people unlikely to improve |

with mental health problems – only to be told this was the wrong approach, as the patients needed to develop 'insight' first, that they were ill and that the mental health team would help them to get better if they just took their medication and did what they were told!

But the recovery approach is gathering momentum. Here is how one psychiatrist buoyantly describes a typical patient encounter:

I work with children and adolescents and I have a long standing interest in OCD [obsessive-compulsive disorder]. I'm passionate about working with young people with OCD to develop coping strategies which will prevent it becoming the life-long handicap that I have seen so often in adults – who never got the help they needed when they first developed symptoms. I never refer to them as *patients* – if I use a word at all, it's *clients*. Typically I start by conveying that OCD is common and that it can be well managed – and sometimes cured. My aim is to convey my belief that this young person can handle it because I believe in their capacity to do so. I ask what *they* want to achieve rather than setting out some lofty treatment plan of my own and sometimes the answers have startled me. I ask what they know about OCD – often it's a surprising amount because they've already been busy googling. I am frank with them about what I've seen work with other young people and invite them to tell me what they think about the various options. Social support is vital and I ask who they believe can be actively on their side. Neuroscience has been helpful, and with the older kids, who are often very bright, I suggest they read Jeffrey Schwartz's fantastic book *Brain Lock*. By the end of the first meeting we have usually sketched out a joint strategy. It's wonderful work – I love it because it succeeds where all that earlier stuff was a resounding failure as far as I can see.

## Working successfully with people who have problems associated with mental illness

In the rest of this chapter we describe some specific techniques and approaches where clinicians have successfully incorporated coaching approaches

### The relationship pillar

The coaching approach is central to working in a recovery-orientated way and, like the recovery approach, is based on assuming a relationship of equals. Everything we have written in earlier chapters, especially in Chapters 2 and 3, applies equally to coaching in a mental health context. Coaching assumes that the service user is resourceful and is competent to manage their life, or will be at some point in the future; it concentrates on identifying and enhancing strengths as opposed to focusing on deficits, and works towards goals primarily set by the service user. Both practitioner and service user play active roles in the relationship, with the preferences of the service user taking a much more central role. Professional expertise is no less valued, but its focus shifts to supporting the service user's recovery process through the assessment, goal-setting and treatment stages.

Warmth, rapport, an authentic welcome, courtesy – these are all vital. The difference they make is enormous:

> My previous psychiatrist had treated me as some kind of curiosity, a specimen, a case, a diagnosis. I was a *depressive paranoiac with latent schizophrenia*. The emphasis was on what medication I had to have and how important it was for me to take it, together with a lot of anxiety about what I might do if I 'got out of control', even though I had never expressed any violence towards myself or anyone else. The new psychiatrist greeted me warmly, sat down with me without a desk between us, smiled, treated me as a fellow adult. I relaxed straight away. I never felt that something was going to be *done* to me. He kept stressing that it was a partnership and that his role was to work with me to get me well again, starting with what I felt were reasonable first steps. I trusted him, I liked him, I believed him and that was the beginning of getting well enough to go back to work.

Never underestimate the impact it can make just to listen without judgement. This psychiatrist describes being able to help a colleague who had been discovered by his boss helplessly weeping and trembling after a period of intense stress at work:

> Anton was one of our facilities managers at the hospital. His boss asked me if I would see him to see if I could offer any help. Anton was very sceptical about how I might help; he was embarrassed that he'd broken down with his boss and was fearful about being seen as 'mad' or 'crazy', but we set up a series of weekly meetings to think about what might have been going on. While most of his unhappiness was to do with day to day work and colleagues, we briefly talked about his childhood and, no surprise here, it included a bullying father. Anton told me how he had been shouting at his staff because of his disappointment that they were not meetings targets and so on, and then began to make the links with his past, saying in a very distraught way, 'I'm afraid of getting just like my father'. Six hour-long meetings was all it needed to give him enough insight to allow him to try a different approach. Listening quietly and asking a few questions was the key to rethinking what was happening in his life. His comment was that he had never made the link between his anger at how he had been treated as a kid and the disappointment he felt at not

being fully on top of his job. By the fourth meeting he had understood that he had choices about how he dealt with his staff just as he had choices about his own feelings and what he did with them. His final comment was, 'This has been so brilliant and it's because you've shown me that you think I'm worth listening to'.

## Using a recovery-orientated assessment process

In a traditional mental health assessment you make a diagnosis and plan treatment. In the recovery approach, the purpose of the assessment is to promote the personal recovery approach of the service user. This involves encouraging the client or service user to develop their own personal meaning from their own experience and having the clinician validate it. In this sense the recovery approach departs significantly from the thinking of some schools of therapy and psychiatry, where part of the practitioner's role is to interpret, analyse and label. As in coaching, this means that it is the individual service user's interpretation that matters, not the clinician's. The assessment is holistic – that is, it is about the whole person not just their illness:

> The nurse talked me through my life so far – it was interesting. He got me to draw it as a chart with dates on one side and then high and low points as a graph. He just nodded as I talked, saying 'uh, go on', or 'that sounds as if it was tough' or 'that sounds as if it was fun'. I'd never seen before that actually a lot of good things had happened as well as a lot of rubbish things.

> I experienced terrible anxiety after my mum died. Suddenly, couldn't shake it off. I expected the psychologist to start on all that Oedipal stuff, how my mum had got it wrong with me and so on, but it was nothing like that. Instead there was a lot about how I was at my best, who else mattered in my life and challenging me every time I said I felt anxious *all the time* – and it was true, it wasn't all the time! Yet I also felt accepted at a very deep level and comforted that a lot of other people had felt swamped the same way I did. I began to feel better straightaway.

### The strengths-based approach to assessment

The traditional mental health assessment process and associated questionnaires are often heavily focused on the negative aspects linked with mental illness, such as identifying symptoms, for example, relating to levels of concentration and energy, sleep patterns, evidence of thought disorder ('delusions', 'hallucinations'), level of drug or alcohol consumption, whether there is a family history of psychiatric illness, assessment of risk of harm to self or others. These are all important areas to assess, but only look at one aspect of the person. Widening the assessment to include a recovery focus can provide a much more holistic picture of the person, identifying and amplifying strengths and resources that the person has and can access.

The paper *100 Ways to Support Recovery*[3] comments: 'One approach is to develop a structured dialogue, equivalent to a mental state examination, to identify a person's strengths, values, coping strategies, dreams, goals and aspirations.' It outlines an assessment of strengths checklist, using parallel categories to the traditional psychiatric history categories familiar to those working in the field of mental health.

## Assessment of strengths

*Current strengths and resources [rather than a history of the presenting illness]*

What keeps you going? Consider spirituality, social roles, cultural/ political identity, self-belief, life skills, toughness, resilience, humour, environmental mastery, support from others, ability to express emotion artistically.

*Personal goals [rather than risk assessment]*

How would you like your life to be different? What are your dreams now? How have they changed?

*Past coping history [rather than past psychiatric history]*

How have you got through the tough times in your life? What supports have you found useful? What do you wish had happened?

*Inherited resources [rather than genetic background]*

Is there any history of high achieving in your family? Any artists, authors, athletes or academics?

*Family environment*

When you were growing up, was there anyone you really admired? What important lessons did you learn during childhood?

*Learning from the past [rather than precipitating events]*

What have past experiences taught you? Are there any positive ways in which you have changed or grown as a person? Consider gratitude, altruism, empathy, compassion, self-acceptance, self-efficacy, meaning.

*Developmental history*

What was life like for you when you were growing up? What did you enjoy? What's your best memory? What skills or abilities did you discover you had?

*Valued social roles [rather than occupational history]*

What would someone you knew really well and liked you say about you? What would you like them to say? How are you useful or of value to others?

*Social supports [rather than relationship history]*

Who do you lean on in times of trouble? Who leans on you?

*Personal history [rather than forensic history, drugs and alcohol]*

What is special about you? Has anyone ever paid you a compliment? What things that you've done or ways that you've behaved make you feel really proud of yourself?

Source: adapted from *100 Ways to Support Recovery*.[3]

## Avoiding pathologizing

Making a diagnosis is one of the acknowledged difficulties of working with people who may have mental health problems and is the subject of much debate, some of it acrimonious, in professional circles.[4]

For example, in the traditional psychiatric approach, people who experience hearing voices that no one else can hear, or who experience extreme feelings of paranoia, would be diagnosed as having a psychotic mental illness. Labelling these experiences as *illness* may be helpful for some people but it may not work for others who do not see themselves as *ill*. Other research[5] has shown that the experience of hearing voices is common, including in people who function normally. Indeed, in some cultures, the experience of hearing voices may be highly valued. For this reason, in this chapter, we refer to *service users* rather than *patients*.

The recovery approach includes caution about labelling. Dr John Launer puts it well in his book, *Narrative-based Primary Care:*[6]

> A diagnosis can in itself be a form of pathologising ... and prolonging the problem. Also, by defining people's symptoms in this way, professionals may be distracted from meeting the patient's wider needs: to make fuller sense of their experiences and to explore their preferred options for change.

An alternative, narrative framework for talking to people who appear to be depressed involves offering them the label of depression without insisting that it has to be relevant or useful. There are questions like:

- 'Would you describe what you are going through as depression?' or
- 'Some doctors would give the name 'depression' to what you are describing – would you find that useful in your own case?'

Such questioning offers patients the landmark of a diagnosis if that is what they wish, without closing down dialogue or stigmatising them if it is not how they view their problems.

## Starting with the service user's frame of reference and goals

Traditional psychiatric services start with the clinician's view of symptoms, especially if the person has what the clinician considers to be a *psychosis*. A psychosis is a condition where the person experiences what psychiatrists term *hallucinations*, *delusions* and *thought disorders*: they lose their grip on reality as it is normally understood. The goal of traditional psychiatry has usually been to provide a diagnosis, such as *schizophrenia* or *bipolar affective disorder*, using traditional diagnostic classification systems, and treatment is aimed at minimizing the symptoms, or facilitating a clinical recovery where the person develops *insight* that their experiences are as a result of their mental illness. In this way mental health diagnoses are usually characterized by lists of symptoms (behaviours or experiences) but have little to say about cause.

In the recovery approach the frame of reference of people accessing mental health services becomes central. The clinician's purpose is to work collaboratively to help identify and work towards goals that have meaning for them:

Alice is a psychiatry trainee who is seeing Dave, a 60-year-old who is profoundly deaf, though he is an excellent lip reader and uses sign language skilfully. Communication is through pen and paper.

Dave has been diagnosed with schizophrenia. He experiences hearing voices which come from outside his head and he attributes them to alien entities which are trying to communicate with him. He is scared that they will harm him and believes that aliens are living all around him as part of an elaborate network where their goal is to work on a computer program that will take control of his brain. Dave has no faith that the psychiatrists or the mental health team caring for him can help him as he knows they don't believe him. He is refusing to take anti-psychotic medication.

In her first meeting with Dave, Alice comes prepared with lots of paper and pens and makes sure she has allowed herself enough time to use them. She asks Dave to give her further details of what he believes about the alien voices, and carefully reads what he has written.

'I do understand', she writes, 'that it must be frightening to be afraid of aliens taking over your brain'. She then asks him what has helped him in the past. He describes having some success once with reducing the voices when he blocked his ears with cotton wool, resulting in him feeling less afraid and more in control as he felt they were less able to access him.

'OK,' writes Alice. 'Let's work on some ways of reducing the noise of the voices.' Together, they explore different ways that this could be achieved. One way was through the use of headphones or earplugs to block his ears, and he was keen to try this. Alice also explains that Dave's medication could be an extra resource as it could help to reduce the noise and number of voices.

Dave agrees to take the medication on a trial basis to see if it has any effect. As the meeting with Alice ends, he looks visibly more relaxed and happy and thanks her for her help and understanding.

Over the following weeks, Dave begins to take the medication, and wears headphones and earplugs intermittently. The voices do indeed reduce and he starts to feel much more confident about himself and his interactions with others as a result.

In this case, the clinician was able to work successfully and in partnership with the service user, using his own frame of reference. Instead of putting her effort into trying to convince Dave that his voices were a fantasy and trying to bully him into taking his medication, Alice was able to promote Dave's belief in his ability to manage his own life. He set his own recovery goal and suggested his own steps towards meeting it.

## The role of language and metaphor

Sometimes a person has been living with mental distress for so long that they have a well-rehearsed narrative about their situation and experiences which may be keeping them stuck. How they tell the story of their own illness, including the language they use, can often be the key to recovery.[7] Working with their language and metaphors is one useful way of helping people work with their own frame of reference, and ultimately to develop their narrative into one which serves their recovery:

Jayne is a 65-year-old with a long-standing diagnosis of depression and who had been treated with fluoxetine for fifteen years. Both she and her family doctor had assumed that maintenance and symptom control were all that could be achieved. When her doctor retired, a new doctor suggested that it might be time to review everything, maybe taking a different approach, and referred her to a colleague with training in cognitive behavioural therapy. This is the practitioner's account of what happened:

I make everything informal – it is mutual first names, all part of the alliance of equals that it's essential to create. I am looking all the time for a way to encourage clients/patients to move away from the familiar drone of a story where they've got stuck, often because they have been given a medically imposed label like 'depression'. We had just six hour-long sessions and I was keen to get the most out of them for her. I could see Jayne was apprehensive, telling me that she feared losing what she called the 'crutch' of the drugs. I asked her how it was a crutch and she said that without it she would be 'lamed' – an interesting metaphor given that if you walk with a crutch you are actually limping.

I asked her to consider what it might be like to walk without the crutch, freely and confidently. For the first time she looked at me properly and gave a little smile.

'Can we play with that as an idea? Just to reassure you, we're not contemplating snatching your crutch away – you can have it as long as you like, but there are other choices and I think our work is to consider them. How do you feel about that?'

She nodded and said she was curious about how it might work.

We began by my asking her to tell me what, if her depression had a name, it would be called. That was easy. She replied instantly, 'Black Blanket'. We discussed how Black Blanket operated: 'He throws a pall over everything, can't see out, feel hopeless, desperate, feel the world would be better off without me' – so these were classic depression symptoms.

Her depression had been triggered by the loss of her senior job fifteen years previously. It sounded like a brutal process: having to apply for her 'own' job and then not getting it after an entire career in the same organization. The organization had made a generous settlement, enough for her to live on, and she had not worked since, doing a lot of what she described as 'sitting about with the blinds pulled down and the lights out', so literally in the dark.

I like the idea of bringing humour to my work so I asked Jayne to tell me Black Blanket's life story as if he was a real person. She was able to do this with no difficulty, describing 'his' close relationship with her – 'my deadly companion' as she put it.

An important part of CBT is restoring the client's belief in their ability to rise above what other people 'do' to them, and part of this is about accepting that usually we have had at least some role in whatever horrible thing has happened. In our third session I asked her what part she felt she might have played in the loss of her job. She confessed that colleagues had sometimes complained that she was 'tough' to work with, though her own view was that all she was doing was pushing for the highest possible standards. 'Yeah, I might have been a bit of a nightmare now I come to think of it...'

In the fourth session I suggested that it might be time to diminish the influence of Black Blanket and asked her to tell me a new story, starting in the present and looking to the future where Black Blanket moved to the outer edge of her social circle and no longer had any ability to throw a pall. She smiled as she did this – again without difficulty.

Between sessions 4 and 5 I asked her to access several heavyweight academic papers on the internet where the effectiveness of SSRIs had been reviewed. We discussed this in the fifth session. We also talked about the importance of pulling friends and family into the process of support. This was another breakthrough: previously she had felt she had to keep everything to herself as a shaming secret, now she decided she would talk openly about her feelings and tell anyone who would listen about Black Blanket and his newly demoted part in her life.

'I see that there's evidence that exercise, daylight plus what we're doing, talking, is just as effective and with no side effects', she observed wryly. We agreed that she would slowly withdraw from the fluoxetine, starting straight away, and would begin a programme of simple daily exercise based on walking.

Session 6 happened around six weeks later: she brought me a little drawing done by her 10-year-old grandson. It was of a coffin, black tulips on top, with underneath, 'RIP Black Blanket'.

This account emphasizes the importance of assuming that there is hope. It is also worth noting that in this story it is the client who is encouraged to do the research into medication rather than having a synthesis of findings presented by the clinician.

### Exploring the look, feel and sound of experience

You can help a client to explore the 'structure' of their experience through using techniques that come from neuro-linguistic programming. One way of doing this is to ask a person who is emotionally distressed where in their body they experience the feeling. Some will point to their head, others to their chest or abdomen, or somewhere else. Focusing on this further, they will very often be able to tell you what shape, size or colour the feeling has, and even whether this 'object' moves, spins, wobbles, is stationary, or has any noise associated with it. Once the structure of the emotion has been established, the person may be able to dissociate themselves from its unhelpful aspects. Understanding that their narrative can have a structure which is separate from the content, and which they can modify, is often hugely empowering as they are no longer a slave to their story, enabling them to move forward. For readers who want to explore this area further, a good starting point is *Magic in Practice* by Garner Thomson and Dr Khalid Khan,[8] which describes these techniques and approaches in more detail, including how to apply them effectively in a health context.

Often you can get remarkably rapid results, as in this account of how a primary care physician was able to help a patient in only two 10-minute consultations:

> Anita, a primary care physician, sees Tony, a 66-year-old retired painter and decorator. He tells her that for the six months since selling his business he has been feeling increasingly anxious, and as a result was finding it difficult to sleep.
>
> 'It's all been so difficult – I think I need sleeping pills'.
>
> 'What's been difficult specifically?' asks Anita.
>
> I have to look after the house, my wife, my health and it's all feeling overwhelming', he says. 'And now the roof's leaking but I can't seem to get round to dealing with it. I've got to look after my wife because she isn't at all well and the anxiety seems to be making everything worse – I feel paralysed with worry.'
>
> 'Where do you feel the worry?' asks Anita
>
> Tony points to his abdomen.
>
> 'Does the worry have a colour?'

Immediately Tony says it is black and in answer to her next question says that it's a spherical shape. Anita then asks Tony to rate his anxiety level on a scale of 1 to 10, with 1 being very comfortable, and 10 being the worst anxiety possible. He describes it as 7. She then guides him through experimenting with the ball, for example by asking him to try pushing away the ball, changing the colour and changing the size.

So what's your worry level now this minute?'

Tony looks astonished. 'It's only 3!' he says.

Tony returns to Anita two weeks later to tell her that he feels much calmer and more relaxed for the first time in six months.

'I've kept practising, like you said. I've started work on the roof,' he says. And it is clear that he no longer wants or needs sleeping tablets.

## Expressing the belief that the service user can get better

Taking a coaching approach also means treating people on the assumption that they have choices, one of which might be that they can choose to get better. The therapist, nurse, doctor or psychologist who encounters such people will also refuse to tiptoe around them as so many have in the past, in the belief that they are too fragile to be treated robustly. We know from countless studies that expectations shape behaviour. For instance, in a much replicated study[9] of how teacher expectations shape pupil performance, teachers were told that a randomly selected group of pupils were 'gifted'. These pupils duly outperformed those who had been assigned equally randomly to the not-so-gifted list. In mental health settings, if you treat people as unable to make decisions they will become unable to make decisions, a theme brilliantly explored in the classic film *One Flew over the Cuckoo's Nest*. The therapist and writer Frank Farrelly wrote entertainingly and thoughtfully about this in his book, *Provocative Therapy*:[10]

> Doom and gloom prognostic statements regarding clients' lack of ability are rampant in the clinical field and are probably much more a reflection of the individual clinician's subjective reaction of helplessness and hopelessness than any objective statement regarding the client. Therapists, like most people, do not like to admit to

failure, and the temptation to practice that alchemy whereby our frustrations and sense of inadequacy is magically transformed into a scientific fact residing in the client is great. 'I failed, therefore you're hopeless. Or 'If I didn't help you then you can't be helped by anyone'…. It is a truism in the clinical field that staff's expectations of hospitalized patients tend to be enacted by the patients. If the staff expects patients to get better, they tend to; and if the staff expects the patients to do nothing, they tend to do exactly that … we must demand more of our clients: in large measure they will behave as they are expected to and are not the equivalent of Dresden china.

This principle applies to most people with mental health problems, some of whom may feel that everyone has given up on them. This may be especially true with the misuse of drugs and alcohol, where disapproval and lack of sympathy may be generated by the belief that such people have brought their problems upon themselves: 'they have made bad judgements and should expect to suffer the consequences'. Drug and alcohol problems may also involve behaviour which breaks the law, as it did with this 23-year-old man:

> Steven had been drinking heavily for many years, but his alcohol consumption got even more out of hand after both his parents died within a few months of each other. His sisters, uncles, aunts and friends begged him to stop. He ignored them all and many cut off contact with him. Waking up hung over every day often made him late for work, and after yet another warning he was fired. Late one Friday night he crashed his car, injuring his girlfriend but escaping with bruises himself. Tests revealed him to be three times over the legal limit. He was prosecuted and convicted, but given a suspended sentence on condition that he entered a treatment programme. Before this could start he survived a suicide attempt that had involved swallowing paracetamol.

> Steven's mental health team connected warmly with him at the same time as challenging his belief that he was worthless, doomed to fail, that he was helpless in the grip of alcohol and that recovery would be hard. Instead they told him that they avoided stigmatizing labels like *alcoholic*, or *suicidal*, agreed with him that he needed to face up to having made some extremely poor choices – and ones that had harmed others as well as

himself – and that they strongly believed in his ability to make better ones. The treatment combined rational emotive therapy with CBT and mindfulness. He was taught ways of challenging the faulty reasoning and black-and-white thinking which had led to his suicide attempt and learned some techniques, based on neuroscience, for managing cravings. Leaving the residential part of the programme, he steadily re-engaged with his family and joined a support group run by SMART Recovery. Apart from a single brief relapse, Steven has now been 'clean' for three years.

## Seeing the service user as a person with a life outside their illness

Traditional approaches to treatment for mental illness have often involved separating the unwell person from their normal environment, including family and friends. Mental illness is the only area of clinical practice where this can be enforced through the law. In contrast, the recovery approach assumes that at some point in the not too distant future, the person will get better and that keeping contact going is crucial. Even when there is serious illness, family and friends need to be consulted:

> Our 17-year-old daughter was clearly ill – out of control manic behaviour, and potentially a danger to herself and others. At first we were relieved when she was admitted to a secure unit for adolescents. I accepted the diagnosis, but my wife was very upset and kept saying that all that our daughter needed was 'peace and some love' and she would be OK. The hospital latched on to my wife because she was able to visit more often than I could. They kept emphasizing how ill our daughter was. After four days we both felt we were not getting anywhere, our opinions were not being heard, nor was our daughter's; the nursing staff just seemed to brush us off and the message was 'trust us, we're the specialists'. We could never get to see the senior doctor. My wife came home on the fifth day saying that our daughter had been physically restrained, she had only been allowed to see her for a few moments and that they were planning to do intra-muscular long-term medication. This was just very, very scary and we felt it was totally wrong. We had not been consulted at all. It was as if

she was in a hospital bubble with an invisible and also a real wall around her.

We protested and arranged immediately for her to be transferred, discovering that actually she had not been put under restraint – it was just one-to-one observation. But she hadn't been refusing medication so the intramuscular strategy was completely inappropriate. We just had to get her out of that hospital, and did.

The new psychiatrist was quite different – he immediately set up a calm, friendly family meeting which included our daughter and our 20-year-old son, listened carefully and asked us what we felt we wanted as the number one priority. Our reply was, 'Please involve us, we know her best'. This was the foundation: then, a week more as an inpatient, a staged return to school, help on briefing the head of sixth form, review of the medication and a gradual return to a normal life. Everything calmed down, the terror of living through a crisis diminished, we were all working together. Just being listened to and the acknowledgement that there was a life and a family involved and that we could be a positive force for good was what made the difference for her and for us.

### Encouraging autonomy

Encouraging autonomy is at the heart of the recovery approach but is not always easy, as a person's self-belief may have been eroded by the symptoms and consequences they experience as a result of mental illness. The reason why this is so challenging is that people with mental health problems so often feel locked into an overwhelming sense of hopelessness.

One way of spotting this is to look out for overgeneralizing which ends with some global condemnation of themselves. In a mentally healthy person this does not happen: there is an unpleasant event which is the cue, perhaps a friend saying something critical, which may trigger a brief feeling of unhappiness, but this is soon put into perspective by remembering happier events and successful relationships (Figure 8.1). When we feel mentally robust we are able to shrug our shoulders and to avoid arriving at the conclusion that we are hopeless failures in every aspect of our lives.

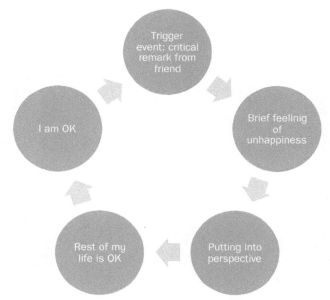

**Figure 8.1** Healthy response to negative comments or events

People who are depressed may constantly find their emotions locked into a cycle where they believe they are defeated and humiliated failures. Attempts to suppress or avoid such feelings seem simply to exacerbate them. For instance, a friend makes a critical comment, this reminds you of other critical comments, a process of generalizing starts which includes believing that critical comments are a pattern and that they define you are a person; people don't love you because you are unlovable and therefore your whole life is a failure (Figure 8.2).

The same phenomenon of entrapment by intrusive thoughts is also characteristic of OCD and in people who become addicted to alcohol or drugs.

### 'Mindfulness' as part of the solution

In its popular modern manifestation, subject of many books, apps, articles, videos and courses, 'mindfulness' is a sophisticated repackaging of a set of techniques and approaches to living which are in all probability as old as humanity. They have appeared over thousands of years

**Figure 8.2** Negative and self-punishing responses to comments or events

as relaxation techniques, yoga, prayer and meditation. Mindfulness, combined with CBT, drugs and other forms of therapy, seems to be a promising route to recovery for many people with depression, suicidal thoughts, addictions and OCD, as well as for people with milder issues of stress or anger management.[11] Mindfulness encourages the belief that you can be in control. It teaches people that their thoughts are just that; they are not commands or compulsions which have to be obeyed. Thoughts can be detached from action. Thoughts are not facts. Thoughts can be separated from emotion by staying in the moment and learning to become aware and to accept what is going on in your body and mind.

In the following example, a client, Jack, and his therapist, Julia, each describes the process:

### Jack (client)

I developed OCD as a teenager, triggered by a guy at my church who told us we'd go to hell if we had wicked thoughts about God; it has plagued my life ever since, and has been a real handicap. I've been on Prozac for years and can't manage without it. I've seen psychiatrists and five different therapists and none really helped, in fact some were awful, for instance just telling me my thoughts were rubbish or trying to force me to do the opposite of the compulsions and making me feel a terrible failure because I couldn't. Now I have a baby daughter and I don't want her to learn this behaviour and I don't want my obsessions ruining my relationship with her and with my wife. Julia has been different. She started by asking me about my successes rather than my failures, then asked me for my goals – number one was to keep the OCD at bay enough to be able to meet deadlines and not drive people crazy because I missed them through obsessions, e.g. being unable to touch my computer because of a 'wicked' thought 'contaminating' what I was typing. In our sessions she's taught me mindfulness techniques and this is the first time I've experienced hope. I realize I have to work at it – and I have. I'm better than I've been for years.

### Julia (therapist)

Jack is a charming and talented 35-year-old strongly motivated to get some control over his OCD. There is a history of OCD in his family – his dad, grandfather, uncle and one nephew have all had it, so there is possibly a genetic thing going on here. Prozac helps him, and at the moment there is no thought of doing without it. I asked his permission to show him mindfulness techniques and we did at least two in each of our six sessions. This included doing an eating meditation, a body scan, a walking meditation, listening to slow classical music, anti-rumination techniques, breathing exercises, identifying typical stimuli and discussing what he found were the best ways of tackling them. We discussed neuroscience findings about new brain pathways and the virtue of practising, and I think that encouraged him to believe he would get better. We reviewed how he had got on with his 'homework' practice at the beginnings of the next sessions.  He is making fabulous progress, mostly I think because for the first time someone has started from where he is, has asked him for his goals and has given him hope as well as some solid scientifically based techniques which are effective.

## Caveats

There are many situations where adopting a coaching approach is not appropriate. For example, people with advanced dementia may have reached the point where all that can be done for them is to contain them with respect and care. There may be severely learning-disabled service users who are vulnerable to abuse and where safeguarding is the primary concern, and others where the opportunities to lead a meaningful life are negligible. But even in such cases there may be opportunities to offer choices, sometimes over some very small things that can make a big difference – for instance, how often therapy sessions occur, when to schedule them, choosing clothing, buying small treats and planning excursions. In most cases there will also be family and carers where a coaching approach will be wholly appropriate.

Note also that simply having the label of a *learning disability* is not a reason to dismiss a coaching approach. The trend is to challenge assumptions that a person with a learning disability has to be supervised and protected to the extent that they are unable to fall in love, have sex lives, enjoy hobbies and leisure activities, live independently, take jobs – and make mistakes, just like anyone else. The same principles of coaching apply as with other mental health services, essentially that the individual is the expert on themselves, can make relationships, can contribute and can be included in the warp and weft of social life without stigma.

## Questions to ask about whether coaching is appropriate

Rather than thinking about whether the specific condition excludes using a coaching approach, we suggest that the questions to ask are whether the coaching principles we describe (see page 30) can apply. There are three that seem especially pertinent (see Table 8.2).

## Does it work?

The values and principles of recovery are being used to guide the development of mental health and substance dependency policies and services across the world including in the USA, Canada, Australia, New Zealand, UK and Ireland.[12] The real challenge will be truly embedding

**Table 8.2 Questions about how far coaching can work in mental health**

| Coaching principle | Comments and questions |
|---|---|
| The client's assumed resourcefulness | Can the person retain and understand information and weigh up pros and cons, taking responsibility for themselves and their choices? Someone with end-stage dementia would not be able to do this, but someone with a new diagnosis of dementia at a very early stage most likely would. Similarly, someone who is acutely intoxicated with drugs or alcohol would not be able to do this, but someone who has a drug problem but has insight into it and is not intoxicated at the time you see them may well respond positively to a coaching approach |
| A relationship of equals based on trust | This is not possible if you think the client is being manipulative and dishonest or if they do not respect or trust you, or if you cannot respect them for some reason – for instance, the nature of their crime if they are in prison |
| Coaching is about change and action | The client needs to want to change. For example, in conditions like anorexia, the person typically lacks insight and does not want to change their behaviour of diet restriction and excessive exercising as they want to continue to lose weight. They may well go to great lengths to deceive professionals and family about the extent of their behaviours.<br>Coaching may work with people who have personality disorders but often at a much slower pace, as behaviours can be so deeply ingrained and such people typically lack insight into the impact on others of what they do |

these values and principles in mental health settings, translating guiding principles into action and into making a genuine culture shift.

The question of how to embed these principles into practice is emerging as an important area for research in the field of mental health. The REFOCUS Programme[13] was a research study which took place in England over five years (2009–14), with the aim of understanding what is meant by personal recovery, and to find effective ways of increasing the recovery support that community-based adult mental health services offer to service users. The intervention developed and implemented in the study consisted of two parts:

- recovery-promoting relationships focusing on the relationships between staff and service users;
- focusing on supporting staff behaviour change relating to the following working practices – understanding values and treatment preferences of service users; assessing strengths; supporting goal striving.

A key component of the intervention for both these parts was to train staff in coaching skills. The REFOCUS intervention was evaluated in a randomized controlled trial[13] which took place in two NHS trusts in England, the South London and Maudsley NHS Trust and the 2gether Partnership NHS Foundation Trust. The study authors recommend the wider use of coaching and the working practices outlined above, in addition to a team-based approach to supporting recovery. You can find further details of this study and the associated outputs (including coaching for recovery training manuals for participants and trainers) on the website www.researchintorecovery.com.

Early research suggests that mindfulness approaches, too, have beneficial impact. Professor Mark Williams, with his colleagues John Teasdale and Zindel Segal, developed mindfulness-based cognitive therapy (MBCT),[14] an eight-week programme of mindfulness training to prevent serious recurrent depression. They showed that MBCT could significantly reduce the rate of relapse in serious recurrent depression. You can find further information about this approach and the evidence that supports it through the continually updated website of the Oxford Mindfulness Centre (oxfordmindfulness.org).

MBCT is now recommended by the UK's National Institute for Health and Clinical Excellence (NICE) as a cost-effective treatment for preventing relapse.[15,16]

## Summary

The recovery approach to mental health draws heavily on coaching principles. It is significantly different from traditional psychiatric approaches in the emphasis it puts on placing the service user at the centre of the action: using their frame of reference, emphasizing their strengths rather than pathologizing weaknesses, working from their goals, emphasizing and building their autonomy and maintaining social contacts with family and community. While there are some caveats about using this approach, the same principles apply as much to mental as to physical health in assuming that, whatever the stage of their illness, most people can benefit from being treated as an equal and playing the central role in the management of their illness.

# References

1. Anthony, W.A. Recovery from mental illness: the guiding vision of the mental health service system in the 1990s. *Psychosocial Rehabilitation Journal* 1993; 16: 11–23.
2. South London and Maudsley NHS Foundation Trust and South West London and St George's Mental Health NHS Trust. *Recovery Is for All: Hope Agency and Opportunity in Psychiatry. A Position Statement by Consultant Psychiatrists.* London: SLAM/SWLSTG; 2010. https://www.rcpsych.ac.uk/pdf/Recovery%20is%20for%20All%20_FINAL%20(2).pdf (accessed 18 August 2015).
3. Slade, M. *100 Ways to Support Recovery: A Guide for Mental Health Professionals*, *Rethink Recovery Series, Vol. 1.* London: Rethink; 2009. http://toronto.cmha.ca/files/2012/11/100-ways-to-support-recovery-Rethink.pdf (accessed 20 August 2015).
4. Callard, F., Bracken, P., David, A.S. and Sartorius, N. Has psychiatric diagnosis labelled rather than enabled patients? *British Medical Journal* 2013; 347: f4312.
5. De Leede-Smith, S. and Barkus, E. A comprehensive review of auditory verbal hallucinations: lifetime prevalence, correlates and mechanisms in healthy and clinical individuals. *Frontiers in Human Neuroscience* 2013; 7: 367.
6. Launer, J. *Narrative-Based Primary Care.* Oxford: Radcliffe Medical Press; 2002.
7. Grove, D. *Philosophy and Principles of Clean Language*; 1998. http://www.clean-language.co.uk/articles/articles/38/1/Philosophy-and-Principles-of-Clean-Language/Page1.html (accessed 3 November 2014).
8. Thomson, G. and Khan, K. *Magic in Practice: Introducing Medical NLP – The Art and Science of Language in Healing and Health* (2nd edition). London: Hammersmith Health Books; 2015.
9. Rosenthal, R. and Jacobson, L. *Pygmalion in the Classroom* (2nd edition). Bancyfelin, Carmarthen: Crown House; 2003.
10. Farrelly, F. and Brandsma, J.M. *Provocative Therapy.* Fort Collins, CO: Shields; 1974.
11. University of Oxford, Oxford Mindfulness Centre. *Research.* http://oxfordmindfulness.org/ (accessed 10 May 2015).
12. Amering, M. and Schmolke, M. *Recovery in Mental Health: Reshaping Scientific and Clinical Responsibilities.* Hoboken, NJ: Wiley; 2009.
13. Institute of Psychiatry, Psychology and Neuroscience, King's College London. *Recovery for Real: A Summary of Findings from the REFOCUS Programme*; 2015. http://www.researchintorecovery.com/files/Recovery%20for%20real%20-%20summary%20of%20REFOCUS%20programme_2.pdf (accessed 10 May 2015).
14. Teasdale, J., Williams, M. and Segal, Z. *The Mindful Way Workbook: An Eight Week Programme to Free Yourself from Depression and Emotional Distress.* New York: Guilford Press; 2014.

15. National Institute for Health and Clinical Excellence. *Depression: The Treatment and Management of Depression in Adults*. Clinical Guideline 90. Manchester: NICE; 2009. http://guidance.nice.org.uk/CG90. (accessed 11 May 2015).

16. National Institute for Health and Clinical Excellence. *Common Mental Health Disorders: Identification and Pathways to Care*. (Clinical Guideline CG123. 2011). http://guidance.nice.org.uk/CG123 (accessed 11 May 2015).

# 9 CONCLUSION: PRESCRIPTION FOR CHANGE

In the introduction to his book, *How Doctors Think*,[1] Dr Jerome Groopman vividly describes a patient who has seemingly exhausted every treatment option. Only in her thirties, she is emaciated, has severe osteoporosis, a perilously low platelet count and her weight has dropped to 82 pounds. For fifteen years she has been treated for bulimia, anorexia, irritable bowel syndrome, depression, anaemia, meningitis, a fracture, plus four admissions to a mental health facility where fruitless attempts were made to help her gain weight under supervision. She has seen close to 30 doctors, including endocrinologists, nutritionists, haematologists, orthopaedists, psychiatrists and psychotherapists. She is living with perpetual nausea, cramps and diarrhoea. Now, a different doctor, a gastroenterologist, approaches this patient in a different way. She is reluctant, she is exhausted, she expects another sermon about bulimia. He sets aside the towering pile of notes and gently asks her to tell her story in her own words, including her emotional responses to the many challenges she has experienced in fifteen years of serious illness, asking a different kind of question where there were no presuppositions, urging her on with brief interventions like 'I'm with you' and 'Go on'. Thanks to this, and then to the further investigations this conversation prompted, the patient was correctly diagnosed with coeliac disease. The well-meant efforts to force thousands of gluten-laden calories a day into her body were exactly what had been destroying it. Within a few weeks she was gaining weight and feeling better than she had for many years.

Dr Groopman comments that doctors are now taught the value of *evidence-based medicine*, often through *decision trees* which in effect are algorithms, a guard against overreliance on the bad old style of thinking based on myth or 'intuition'. But, as he says:

> It was her words that led Falchuk [her gastroenterologist] to correctly diagnose her illness and save her life. While modern medicine is aided by a dazzling array of technologies, like high-resolution MRI scans and pinpoint DNA analysis, language is still the bedrock of clinical practice.

This doctor was in effect using a coaching approach, asking brief, focused questions, encouraging the patient to talk, seeking first to understand her experience through the language she was using and the story she was telling, including its emotional dimensions. This released him from the rigid thinking style that so many of his predecessors had deployed and which, had it continued, would have led eventually to this patient's death.

Our main purpose in writing this book is to define and introduce you to the power of coaching in clinical consultations. In this final chapter we examine some of the common traps to implementing a coaching approach, look at some of the doubts which may still be in your mind, and discuss how to get better at it.

## Blaming the patient

Despite the impressive authority that clinical training gives, vast numbers of patients wriggle away from clinician control. They do not take their medication, they say yes when they mean no or no when they mean yes, they argue, they obfuscate, they do not agree that their problems merit attention, they do not attend their appointments, they refuse screening, they insist on trying unproven or discredited herbal remedies for life-threatening diseases – the list of ways in which patients sabotage clinicians is literally endless.

Faced with apparently non-compliant patient behaviour, we notice that many clinicians get exasperated, upset and worried (see Chapter 4). In the face of their own anxiety and frustration, they give in to the temptation to blame the patient. This may take two forms, sometimes present simultaneously. First, where self-harm is evident – such as with attempted suicides, anorexia, 'cutting', accidents that have resulted from alcohol consumption and so on – there may be less tolerance and more impatience observable in clinician behaviour. Research[2] on the treatment of young people who have self-harmed suggests that barely controlled disapproval is evident in many such clinician–patient conversations, but there is no reason to suppose that the same rush to irritation is not present in other, less obvious scenarios where the patient has seemingly been the primary player in their own problem. Secondly, where the patient's lack of compliance is less plain, for instance, a diabetic patient who takes their medication haphazardly or a morbidly obese patient who appears to believe that their weight is within the normal limits, the phrase we hear constantly is that these patients are 'in denial', in other words that it is the patients' fault.

## Being in denial?

From running courses for clinicians we recall the typical scenarios and language they have used to describe their frustrating interactions with such patients:

> I asked why he had attempted suicide. He just shrugged his shoulders and said 'I dunno, it all felt like it was too much'. I asked what was too much. Again, shrug. 'I dunno.'

> 'You're not coming for regular checks on your blood pressure – why?' Silence. Just wouldn't say. Felt like screaming. 'You're in denial about your hypertension!'

> Inexplicable: like watching a slow car crash when someone refuses to moderate their drinking – I mean a huge amount of vodka a day? Come on. You've got to see that you're an alcoholic, but he couldn't! Denial? Yeah, in spades!

> Told the patient that her BMI was 38 and that she was heading for an early grave. No reply. I said, 'You are very, very overweight'. Patient looked away: these patients deny they are fat! What are you to do with them?

> This isn't why I came into medicine: to preside over a death wish in young girls who can't see that their refusal to eat is killing them!

## Challenging yourself

We are reminded here of the wise words of Milton Erikson, a gifted psychotherapist who once commented that there is no such thing as a difficult patient, only an inflexible therapist. It is perfectly true that human beings have an infinite capacity for self-delusion, for instance about how slim we are, how hooked we are on cigarettes, how reliant on alcohol, how attractive we are, how much any of our palpably bad habits will have long- or short-term impact.

But 'denial' is not a fixed personality trait; it is the direct result of defending your self-esteem against what you perceive to be an attack, sometimes multiple attacks over decades, on your way of life or on who you feel you really are. A patient whom you perceive to be 'in denial' is actually telling you as clearly as possible that they have not felt heard.

When faced with 'I don't know' or mute resistance or arguing, our own first thoughts in such situations are to challenge ourselves with any one or more of the following:

● I'm obviously out of rapport with this patient and I need to get back into it straight away, perhaps through a summary. Check my body language – what's it telling me?
● This patient can't be open with me: how can I make it possible for this to happen?
● I've fallen back into lecturing and telling.
● I've asked the wrong question.
● What are the patient's feelings here? I'm overconcentrating on the facts!
● I'm missing something important. I need to go back a step.

The response to apparent patient stubbornness is to recognize that patients may be in a different place psychologically and physically from the one you assume – or that you think is desirable. If they have just had surgery, they may be preoccupied with pain and with how long their recovery will take. A patient who has just given birth may be overcome by the emotional impact of the experience and may not be in the right place for a necessary discussion about future contraception. If a patient has just experienced the breakdown of an important relationship he may be far more worried about that than about how many cigarettes he is smoking. Where they have just been made redundant, how to get another job may be a patient's primary preoccupation, not whether or not to have an operation. They may not share your beliefs about prevention being better than cure; they may not agree about the seriousness of their situation because they may come from a culture which sees these things differently. The solution, as ever, is to step up the rapport, to ask what they want and to ask the questions which will make their inner world more visible.

It is also worth asking if there is some *projection* going on here (see also page 74). Projection is the psychological phenomenon which occurs when we see something in others which we know, or fear, could be true of us. It is too painful to contemplate our own failings so we project them on to others. An example would be a doctor who regularly relies on alcohol to self-soothe after a stressful day but who is heavily critical of patients who abuse alcohol. So a further useful question might be:

● Is my response to this patient a little extreme? If so, what is this telling me about myself?

## Common questions and doubts

As a healthcare professional reading this book, you may still be asking yourself how far a coaching approach is going to be useful to you with the types of patient you see from day to day. There is more on all these topics in earlier chapters, but we summarize here the main questions that we find clinicians ask when they are first introduced to coaching skills.

*Will I have enough time to use coaching skills with my patients?*

Many clinicians work in healthcare settings where a 10-minute consultation is the norm, so how could there be time to incorporate this new approach? In practice, however, what many participants report, after undertaking some training, is that they have immediately been able to use focused elements of what they have learnt. For example, they have tried setting the agenda for the consultation, asking the patient to identify at the start what they are hoping to discuss, ensuring that best use is made of the limited time available; or asking the patient coaching-style questions such as what they would like ideally, what is stopping them achieving what they want to achieve, what is within their control, what their next step will be. Sometimes, simply summarizing has been a powerful lever towards helping a patient order their thoughts and make sense of their situation.

Clinicians report, often with surprise, that tailoring their consultations to the individual patient does not take more time, and in many instances can save time, especially when you identify and agree the focus early on. These anecdotal experiences are supported by the findings of a recent study.[3] We have found time and again that the most effective and efficient conversations are not the ones which take the longest. Instead they are the ones where the healthcare professional believes in the patient's own resourcefulness, and their attention is fully directed to the patient, ever alert not only to the cues the patient is offering but also to their own inner voice, enabling them to ask the right question or to offer the right feedback at the right time to help move the patient forward. That powerful question may take just seconds to ask, but the impact on the patient may be immense.

Although the 10-minute consultation may be the most common, there are many other circumstances where more time is available. For instance, in many hospitals a 30-minute appointment will be standard for a newly referred patient. As well as taking a history and assessing all the available data, this will give ample scope for a coaching approach to be used throughout the consultation. Even in a more pressured environment, a single 10-minute appointment may be just one in a series, giving more time to build the relationship.

> *You seem to encourage patients to ramble on with their stories. Isn't this a luxury when we are so time-poor?*

This is a variant of the preceding question and is often raised when we discuss and demonstrate the value of listening rather than talking. Sometimes it is true that a patient's situation is so complex that he or she will need a longer appointment. But the answer to the question is that if the patient is *rambling on* it is not a true coaching conversation. A coaching-style consultation always has a goal, a mid-point and an end point where some action is agreed. If the patient is controlling the conversation as well as telling their story then you will both end up getting nowhere. As the practitioner, you are the one with responsibility for the *process framework* of the consultation rather than its *content*, for instance, creating rapport, judging what question to ask, asking for the patient's agenda, keeping an eye on the time, listening carefully to the language they are using and, yes, knowing when to interrupt for the benefit of both parties. This is why the skill of summarizing seamlessly (see page 66) is so vital as it can be a respectful way of maintaining rapport while simultaneously managing the discussion.

*Tick-box mania: how can I use this approach when the system demands that I interrogate patients about their blood pressure, weight or smoking?*

The more anxiety there is about public health, the more likely it is that clinicians will be encouraged to ask questions which come from a government agenda rather than from the patient. Sometimes there will be financial incentives for doing so. This has sometimes been dubbed *surveillance medicine*, a term which conveys the intense dislike for it that so many clinicians feel.

An overemphasis on ticking boxes is a well-recognized cause of disillusionment and burnout in healthcare practitioners. We find in actuality that the coaching approach and the tick-box approach are not mutually exclusive. You do not need to interrogate patients. When you raise questions of weight, smoking or blood pressure you can do it in a way which respects the patient's autonomy by focusing on the health outcomes that matter to them. The emphasis now is more on outcome than on process measures – for instance, whether a blood pressure target has actually been met rather than whether you have measured the patient's blood pressure. This in its turn puts the emphasis on the most effective way of achieving the outcome. Patient-reported outcome measures (PROMs)[4] are also increasingly being used as a measure of quality in healthcare. Both of these are far more likely to be achieved if you use a coaching approach.

*Isn't this coaching thing just a trick?*

When clinicians begin to realize the power of coaching, they sometimes ask whether it is a technique that can be switched on and off in order to manipulate patients. We cannot emphasize strongly enough that this is not the case. Coaching recognizes that ultimately patients cannot be forced to do anything, that it is the patient who knows themselves best and who lives with the results of any clinical intervention. When you use a coaching approach with patients you are open and undefended; you do not have some fixed end in view because you do not know how the conversation will go. Coaching is a genuinely collaborative process which acknowledges the power of the patient. It is the opposite of manipulative. Once coaching skills are learnt, our experience is that they filter into every exchange, not just with patients but as a rewarding and respectful method of interacting in everyday life.

*I already know how to do this – I've trained in communication skills. Isn't that the same thing?*

Many healthcare professionals have undergone some level of communication training at either undergraduate or postgraduate level or both, and this training can range from a focus on specific skills such as building rapport to learning patient-centred consultation models. A helpful summary of these models can be found in Ramesh Mehay's book.[5] A coaching for health approach may include elements of all such models.

However, far from being just another consultation model, we prefer to see coaching for health as a mindset, whereby right from the start there is a sense of a true clinician–patient partnership, where the patient remains the expert on themselves and the clinician's role is primarily one of facilitation, supporting the patient to identify and achieve the healthcare outcomes that are meaningful to them. This could often involve an element of providing information and of ensuring that any interventions take local and national guidelines and the current evidence base into account.

*I mentor trainees and I train students, so how is this different?*

Mentoring and training are close cousins to coaching but not the same. When you are in a mentoring or training role you may call on many of the same skills as the ones necessary for coaching. But you control the agenda for training and mentoring conversations; you are working to exacting standards set by accrediting and licensing bodies, and part of your role is to ensure that these standards are maintained. Overall you therefore have more power than the trainee or mentee. This is significantly different from coaching, where the emphasis is on a relationship of equals.

*I can think of several patients who are not in a resourceful state and not able to take responsibility for their own health. How is a coaching approach relevant for them?*

There will be many situations where coaching is inappropriate – for example, the acutely psychotic patient, the patient with an advanced dementia, the patient in a reduced state of consciousness. Similarly, there will be occasions where it is essential for tests and scans to be ordered, critical information to be offered and your own concerns to be raised openly.

Coaching is not a panacea to be used indiscriminately in every healthcare encounter. Yet even in situations where the patient is unable to make their own decisions, you will be communicating with relatives and carers, and a coaching approach can be invaluable in such conversations.

*Coaching seems to have a future focus, but my patients are at the end stages of their lives.*

We have sometimes been asked by palliative care clinicians whether it is appropriate to use a future-focused approach like coaching with patients who may have a very limited life expectancy. We have been heartened by the feedback we have had from these clinicians once they have completed some training and have tried these approaches with patients who may not have long to live. They have found it has enabled them to have powerful conversations with their patients about what they actually want to achieve in the time they do have left, for themselves and their families, and to empower them to identify and take the steps needed to make this happen.

The writer and surgeon Atul Gawande (see also pages 10, 45 and 116) devotes a large part of his book, *Being Mortal*,[6] to this question, including a moving account of his father's terminal illness and death. He describes his shock, later turning to relief, at the direct but sensitive approach of a local hospice nurse, of whom, as he admits, he had had low expectations. But she asked his father questions in a way that no one in the family had been able to do, as in this example:

Then she asked, 'What funeral home do you want to use? And I was divided between shock – are we really having this conversation? – and reassurance at how normal and routine it was to her.

'Jagers' he said without hesitation. He'd been thinking about it all along, I realized. My father was calm.

The ability of this nurse to listen and to ask well-chosen questions drew out from his father that what mattered to him was minimizing pain and grogginess along with lessening the risk of falls, as well as being able to communicate and socialize. In his last weeks he was able to attend a convocation at which his son would be giving the address, walking very slowly over a distance he had not achieved for half a year, to join the families in the stands:

> I was almost overcome just witnessing it. Here is what a differ-ent kind of care – a different kind of medicine – makes possible, I thought to myself. Here is what having a hard conversation can do.

These vital conversations can seem difficult, or sometimes taboo, and may not be initiated by the patient or their families, from fear of caus-ing further upset or awkwardness. The clinician's skill in facilitating these conversations can be invaluable for all concerned in helping them move forward in an open, honest and constructive way. We believe that the potential role of coaching in palliative care would make an impor-tant and fascinating topic for further research as there is currently little in the literature exploring it.

*Surely many patients just want to be told what to do?*

Several factors over the last few decades have changed the health-care climate. We are in a field where patients have easy access to healthcare information over the internet, there is greater media coverage and transparency, and the traditional patriarchal clini-cian–patient relationship no longer meets the requirements of the times. A new approach to consulting and communication is needed, one which puts the patient truly at the centre of their own healthcare. In recent years, much has been made politically of the notion of *patient choice*. But in practice, this is only mean-ingful if the patient is facilitated in making an informed choice, one which takes their individual current life context into account alongside any available evidence base, and where the patient has genuine ownership of that choice.

A growing body of evidence indicates that a new type of patient is emerging. Tom Ferguson coined the term 'e-patients' to describe individuals who are 'equipped, enabled, empowered and engaged' in their health and healthcare decisions. He sees healthcare as an equal partnership between e-patients and health professionals and systems that support them.[7]

Evidence continues to accumulate on the benefits of patient-centred communication generally, and a full review of this is outside the scope of this book. But research from around the world indicates that people want to be more involved in their care, that they value a person-centred consultation style and communication,[8-11] and that many want more involvement in decisions about their treatment and care.[12] There is also compelling evidence that a person-centred style of communication can improve patient health outcomes.[13-15]

Coaching for health is an inherently patient-centred approach which supports patient empowerment, involvement and activation, putting patients at the centre of care and decisions.[16]

*Isn't this approach only useful for educated patients and those who speak good English?*

This is another area that would benefit from further research, as little exists currently in the literature. We have heard from many colleagues who work in areas with low literacy rates and who have used coaching successfully with patients who speak either no or very little English (there is more on this in Chapter 7). It is easy to make assumptions about what these patients may or may not want or be capable of. And if these assumptions mean that we do not ask the patients directly, their voices may never be heard. The results of using an empowering approach can be dramatic.

*Can you use this skill with children?*

Many of the paediatricians and general practitioners attending our courses regularly report on the effectiveness of using coaching for health skills with children and their families. With very young children, the most basic skills of effective rapport-building, eye contact, speaking to them at their level, can be as powerful as they are with adults. Children have rich imaginations, and a question relating to their health issue along the lines of 'if a fairy magically appeared and granted you three wishes, what would you wish for?', for example, can a powerful way of identifying what is really important to the child, enabling the clinician to tailor explanations and management plans appropriately.

*What about my duty of care to the patient?*

Healthcare professionals owe a duty of care to the patient. It is a professional and a legal obligation. Using a coaching approach does not in any way lessen your duty of care to your patient or to the professional and clinical standards that you would normally apply in your interactions with them. If you have vital information to share with them or a clinical opinion that it is important for them to hear, you will still offer it. The question is only how you offer it (there is more on this in Chapter 5). A coaching for health approach will increase the effectiveness of your communication with your patients, with the ultimate goal of supporting them to achieve the healthcare outcomes that matter most to them.

Duty of care relates directly to our perception our clinical roles. Here are some common responses that we have heard from clinicians when asked about their role:

My role is to help the patient.

I am responsible for my patients.

I have to look after my patients because they are incapable of looking after themselves.

There is a difference between the duty of care and taking on a parental or guiding role with patients. When we place ourselves as the *helper* or *rescuer* of the patient, we may be automatically putting the patient in a *victim* role, triggering an unhealthy power dynamic between clinician and patient, inadvertently disempowering them, making decisions on their behalf and then 'persuading' them to go along with what we 'strongly recommend'. In doing this, we deny them the control and responsibility for their health while also setting ourselves up for failure. So if, for example, our 'help' is ineffective, unwanted or rejected, we then become responsible for the patient's continuing health issues. By not allowing patients to make truly informed decisions about their healthcare, taking into account their own life context, which they are in a position to understand better than anyone else, we have to question whether we are really fulfilling our duty of care to patients (see also page 202). By using a mindset that enables the patient to take responsibility for their health, we adopt an approach where we are far more likely to enable and support patients to make the decisions that are best for them as well as ensuring that we maintain our duty of care.

## Getting better at coaching

For all that coaching skills can look simple, our own experience is that these skills fall into the category of *simple but not easy*. You cannot learn how to do it from a book, a video, an online article, a webinar or an introductory lecture, useful though all of these can be. Learning what coaching for health *is* can be valuable but it is different in style and purpose from learning the skills and getting feedback on how you are doing.

When you see a skilled coaching practitioner at work it looks effortless, but it is the effortlessness achieved by training and intensive feedback followed by a great deal of disciplined, mindful practice and supervision. In everyday life, most of us have no idea how poor our listening skills are, how readily we interrupt or queue to speak, how eager we are to offer our own opinions or how much we need to be right. It takes commitment, time and minimally several days of intensive face-to-face training plus subsequent supervision and practice to learn how to overcome the typically ingrained habits which get in the way.

### The ladder of competence

At first it is normal to feel self-conscious about using coaching skills. It seems *clunky*, unnatural. It can help to remember the *ladder of competence* (which was developed from Noel Lynch's model of the four stages of learning),[17] with each 'rung' representing a necessary phase of learning:

*Unconscious incompetence*: we are unaware of our own bad habits and levels of ineptitude.

*Conscious incompetence*: it is embarrassing to face up to how incompetent we are; the task of learning feels impossible, it's all too difficult; it all has to be practised simultaneously, how will that ever be possible?

*Conscious competence*: we know what the skills are and can use them but it is effortful to remember them (the *clunky* phase); we slip back easily into old ways, but now at least we recognize what these are.

*Unconscious competence*: we have internalized the skills and no longer have to struggle to use them.

Acquiring any worthwhile and complex skill, which is what coaching is, will involve passing through each of these phases. It is impossible to go immediately from unconscious incompetence to conscious competence. However, training can make the process speedier and smoother – as long as it involves a high level of practice and feedback with plenty of follow-up after trying the skills away from the sheltered environment of a course.

## How system changes could help

The people who attend our courses are enthusiastic volunteers; often they have already had some exposure to the ideas behind coaching for health and are interested enough to put themselves through rigorous further learning. We are well aware that many will go back to their hospitals or practices as the sole ambassador for an approach which some of their colleagues will find unfamiliar and challenging. It all becomes so much easier when you are working in an environment where there is systemic support, for instance for a different approach to initial assessments, for patient education groups which are facilitative and not didactic, for a rolling programme of training workshops open to people from every clinical discipline and not just the doctors, for team discussions where successes can be shared and failures explored in a non-judgemental way. We would like to see coaching embedded in the initial training of all healthcare students and young postgraduates where experienced supervisors could observe and offer feedback on their consultations as well as introducing the ideas through conferences and training courses for experienced clinicians.

The need to make a systemic shift is well acknowledged through calls for action on patient empowerment from many hundreds of different bodies worldwide: universities, government departments, professional associations and patient interest groups. But coaching for health still needs powerful champions to bring it all together. It will all be so much easier when the whole system endorses the values and skills of coaching and with serious money to back it. How to do this is beyond our scope in this book but we are hopeful that that there is unstoppable momentum for making it happen.

## Finally

Clinicians are and always will be up against the limitations of human biology. The power we have to stretch life and to fight disease is awesome but it is finite. In the end the clinician role is more than just helping patients to survive, it is about the whole of life and quality of life; it is about well-being, autonomy, happiness and the power of choice. That is where coaching can add so much not just to patients but to the increased satisfaction that we, as clinicians, are likely to get from our work.

## References

1. Groopman, J. *How Doctors Think*. Boston: Mariner Books; 2007.
2. Lilley, R., Owens, D. *et al.* Hospital care and repetition following self-harm: multi-centre comparison of self-poisoning and self-injury. *British Journal of Psychiatry* 2008; 192: 440–445.
3. Ahluwalia, S., De Silva, D., Kumar, S., Viney, R. and Chana, N. Teaching GP trainees to use health coaching in consultations with patients: evaluation of a pilot study. *Education for Primary Care* 2013; 24(6): 418–426.
4. Devlin, N.J. and Appleby, J. *Getting the Most out of PROMs*. London: King's Fund; 2010. https://www.kingsfund.org.uk/sites/files/kf/Getting-the-most-out-of-PROMs-Nancy-Devlin-John-Appleby-Kings-Fund-March-2010.pdf (accessed 20 February 2015).
5. Mehay, R (ed.). *The Essential Handbook for GP Training and Education*. London: Radcliffe Publishing; 2012.
6. Gawande, A. *Being Mortal: Medicine and What Matters in the End*. New York: Metropolitan Books; 2014.
7. Ferguson, T. e-Patients Scholars Working Group. *e-Patients: How They Can Help Us Heal Health Care*; 2007. http://e-patients.net/e-Patients_White_Paper.pdf (accessed 13 October 2014).
8. Campos, D.C. and Graveto, J.M. The role of nurses and patients' involvement in the clinical decision-making process. *Revista Latino-Americana de Enfermagem* 2009; 17(6): 1065–1070.
9. Baars, J.E., Markus, T., Kuipers, E.J. *et al.* Patients' preferences regarding shared decision-making in the treatment of inflammatory bowel disease: results from a patient-empowerment study. *Digestion* 2010; 81(2): 113–119.
10. Schattner, A., Bronstein, A. and Jellin, N. Information and shared decision-making are top patients' priorities. *BMC Health Services Research* 2006; 6: 21.

11. Loh, A., Kremer, N., Giersdorf, N., Jahn, H. *et al.* Information and participation interests of patients with depression in clinical decision making in primary care. *Zeitschrift für Ärztliche Fortbildung und Qualitätssicherung* 2004; 98(2): 101–107.

12. Sizmur, S. and Redding, D. *Key Domains of the Experience of Hospital Outpatients*. Discussion Paper 2. Oxford: Picker Institute Europe; 2010.

13. Lewin, S.A., Skea, Z.C., Entwistle, V., Zwarenstein, M. and Dick, J. Interventions for providers to promote a patient-centred approach in clinical consultations. *Cochrane Database of Systematic Reviews* 2001; (4): CD003267.

14. McKinstry, B., Ashcroft, R.E., Car, J., Freeman, G.K. and Sheikh, A. Interventions for improving patients' trust in doctors and groups of doctors. *Cochrane Database of Systematic Reviews* 2006; (3): CD004134.

15. Mead, N. and Bower, P. Patient-centred consultations and outcomes in primary care: a review of the literature. *Patient Education and Counseling* 2002; 48(1): 51–61.

16. Butterworth, S. Health-coaching strategies to improve patient-centered outcomes. *Journal of the American Osteopathic Association* 2010; 110(4 Suppl 5): eS12–4.

17. Adams, L. *Learning a New Skill Is Easier Said Than Done*; 2011. http://www.gordontraining.com/free-workplace-articles/learning-a-new-skill-is-easier-said-than-done/ (accessed 20 February 2015).

# INDEX

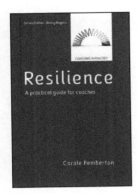

**Resilience**
A practical guide for coaches

Carole Pemberton

ISBN: 978-0-335-26374-5 (Paperback)
eBook: 978-0-335-26375-2
2015

*Resilience: A Guide for Coaches* is based on the author's experience as an expert executive and career coach. Inspired by her own research with individuals who have lost their resilience; it provides key insights from psychology, case study evidence and tools for coaches to work with on resilience issues.

**Practicing or training coaches can gain:**

- An understanding of what resilience is, and what separates it from burnout and trauma
- A range of approaches that they can use in working with resilience issues
- A better understanding of the their ownresilience

www.openup.co.uk